Montreal at the Crossroads

by Donna Gabeline
Dane Lanken
Gordon Pape

 Harvest House / Montreal

ACKNOWLEDGMENTS

Portions of this book originally appeared in
The Gazette. The authors gratefully acknowledge
the cooperation of *The Gazette* management in
allowing this material to be reproduced here.
We also wish to thank the photographers of
The Gazette Photo Service for permitting us to
reproduce their film record of Montreal in
evolution. The book has been published with
the help of a grant from the Social Science Research Council of Canada, using funds provided
by the Canada Council.

THE AUTHORS
Donna Gabeline and Dane Lanken are reporters
for *The Gazette*.
At the time of writing, Gordon Pape was
Associate Editor of *The Gazette*. He is now
Assistant to the Publisher of the *Financial Times
of Canada*.

Design by Sue Scott
Cover photo: Victorian greystones on Crescent
Street by Michael Dugas of *The Gazette*.

Printed and bound in Canada.

To the people of Montreal.

Table of Contents

Chapter One

Someplace Has to Feel Like Home

"Montreal will be the first city of the 21st century."
—Jean Drapeau

Montreal is in the midst of a period of runaway development that is surpassing even the spectacular growth of the early 1960's.

New high-rise towers are going up on almost every corner in the downtown area. Old buildings are falling before bulldozers and wreckers' balls almost daily.

Within a decade, much of the city core will be almost unrecognizable.

Mayor Jean Drapeau says that what is happening right now will make Montreal the world's first city within 15 years. He takes much of the credit himself: "If things happen in this city, it is because I capture the real wishes and needs of the people at large."

Toronto alderman William Kilbourn takes a different view, however. He sees what is happening in Montreal as "not galloping progress but galloping destruction" and he asks Montrealers: "Do you really want to go the way of New York and Detroit?"

Montreal is at the crossroads in its development as a city. The direction the present building boom takes and the controls that are placed on it will determine what kind of environment will face the Montrealers of the 21st century.

The present course of events has many people worried.

The Montreal *Gazette* warned editorially in March, 1974, that the city is facing "a genuine crisis of urban politics."

"It is a crisis of civic will, of whether citizens are going to participate in the growth of their city or let it go by default," the paper said.

"Only by deformation is it a confrontation between developer and conservationist, for the ordinary citizen remains in favor of healthy growth. But it could develop into a confrontation if the land speculators, builders, and the business and industrial constituency they serve continue to bulldoze their way through all values but material values—values like neighborliness, privacy, tranquility, pleasing surroundings, aesthetic attraction, variety, individuality, and enjoyment of land, air and water in their natural state."

Much of old Montreal has already been lost, but there is still something to be saved. Says Prof. Melvin Charney of the University of Montreal's School of Architecture: "The next few years will decide whether this is to become another homogenized North American city, or whether it will retain its human scale. If the city is going to retain a human scale, we are going to have to stop tearing it apart."

The disturbing thing to many planners and urban experts is that Montreal's new development boom is taking place in a haphazard, uncoordinated way, without central planning or guidance.

"The downtown is up for grabs," says Anshel Melamed, an official in the planning section of Montreal's Housing and Planning Department.

"Right now Montreal is a very pleasant city to live in, despite some bad elements. But if we keep going the way of progress, it will be unbearable."

The professional developers, big and small, are converging on Montreal in unprecedented numbers.

Hutchison Street greystones

11

"Since the new laws were passed in Toronto, all the developers have been moving to Montreal," says Richard Glickman, assistant to the president of Central Holdings, a large builder of high-rises and apartment complexes.

"Toronto was a boom town, there were buildings going up everywhere. Montreal has reacted like an elastic. It was held back for so long; now it has snapped. You're going to see high-rises from the Forum all the way to Amherst."

The impact of the developers' invasion is visible everywhere in the city.

Some of Montreal's finest 19th century buildings are in danger or have already been destroyed, often to be replaced with shoddily-built apartment blocks that charge high rents now but which urbanists predict will become the slums of the next generation.

Long-established communities like Milton-Park and St. Jacques have been broken up by huge redevelopment schemes, and their residents scattered. Other communities, like Chinatown and the Main, are in imminent danger.

Gatherings of people such as these are vital to the fabric and excitement of any city.

"The human touch is still here," says Peter Vizel, founder of the Save the Main Movement.

"You can get things here you can't get anywhere else. There are stores with selections of cheese and coffee that can compete with any. How many places do you know where you can still get fresh cold cuts—not eight slices in a plastic wrapper? You can still buy hot bread at Levine's bakery."

Despite the spirited defense of residents, many of the old communities are being wiped out. As they vanish, the character of the city changes.

"Montreal is like a forest which has taken a long time to grow," says Melvin Charney. "Now it is being cut down and there is no reforestation program."

In recent years, much of the charm that used to characterize Stanley, Drummond, Mountain and Bishop streets has been destroyed by new development. Crescent St. still retains most of its old houses with their fashion boutiques, bars and intimate restaurants, but it too has been coming under development pressure. Only intervention by City Hall in the summer of 1974 has provided much-needed breathing space.

The solidly-built, low-rise houses and apartment blocks just west of Guy between Dorchester and Sherbrooke are giving way to high-rises which architect Michael Fish, of the Save Montreal Movement, describes as being "as bad as anything in the world."

Sherbrooke St. is being transformed from a gracious, tree-lined residential street and shopping promenade into a series of towers. Says David Carter, director of the Montreal Museum of Fine Arts: "It is being turned into a high-rise canyon where the sun never penetrates and the wind makes being outside extremely unpleasant."

McGill University, while preserving some of its fine 19th century pavilions, has built up much of the green space that made its campus a haven in the center of the city. It has also torn down many fine old buildings on University, Redpath and Sherbrooke streets and replaced them with featureless modern structures.

"Our present development system gives all the answers in terms of dollars and cents," says Carter. "Until the city decides to give priority to other values, this situation will not change."

That does not mean all new development is bad, however—far from it.

"Place Ville Marie and other developments of that period were remarkably advantageous to the city and its citizens in general," says architect Ray Affleck. "They added real value and since they were built on what were holes in the ground, they didn't take anything away."

Montreal's city center has become more vital, says Kurt Jonassohn, a sociology professor at Sir George Willams campus of Concordia University.

"Look at the subway. The Toronto subway was built from a purely functional point of view. In Montreal, they had a different architect for each station and the subway was built to appeal to people's taste, with some cultural notion of elegance."

Some of the new buildings being planned for the McGill College Ave. area between St. Catherine and Sherbrooke streets are as exciting in their conceptual form as the best of the 1960's.

Developer extraordinaire Vincent Ponte, probably the world's leading expert on the multi-level city, predicts that within 10 years Montreal's underground city will extend all the way from below St. James St. in the south to the McGill University campus in the north, and from The Bay in the east to the Peel Metro station in the west.

He talks enthusiastically of six to seven miles of underground walkways which will link together 400 shops and boutiques, 10,000 underground parking spaces, 5,000 hotel rooms, 30 to 40 restaurants, 10 cinemas, two train stations, the Stock Exchange and the Metro.

"When it is completed it will be eight times bigger than the nearest comparable thing in the world, which is New York's Rockefeller Center," he says.

"This is our answer to congestion, our answer to weather, and our answer to creating a new environment in a 21st century city."

But Ponte's vision of a vast underground city unmatched in the world doesn't allay many of the concerns about the way in which the face of Montreal is changing.

"Underground cities are all right, but we are not troglodytes," says David Carter. "We have to come out into the air once in a while."

It is what we see when we do emerge from underground that is bothering many planners. They are worried about the quality of much of the architecture that is going up, about people being driven out of the center of the city as residential areas are replaced by office blocks, about growing traffic congestion, about the tendency to hastily bulldoze solid older buildings without serious consideration as to whether they might be given new life, about the shortage of green space, and about the soulless nature of much of the new construction.

"Montreal lacks a visionary, comprehensive plan," says architect and town planner Jean-Claude LeHaye, whose report on a comprehensive land-use program was shelved by the provincial government a decade ago as being too avant-garde.

"We must develop the downtown area as compactly as possible so as to prevent sprawl such as we have seen in Toronto.

"Not enough people live in the center of the city. They are being driven out and most streets are dead at night. The city is far from being as lively as the hearts of cities like London and Paris.

"We need to discourage traffic, encourage public transportation and develop a pedestrian circulation system that will encourage people to walk on the streets. Right now the city is like a desert."

None of this is going to happen without strong action from City Hall. As C.M. Drury, federal Public Works Minister, puts it: "Mayor Drapeau's desires, good or ill, will be fulfilled."

The Mayor's main interests through most of his period in office have been in promoting grandiose projects like Expo 67, the Metro, major league baseball and the Olympics. Critics say he is less concerned with more mundane problems like public housing, pollution control and sewage disposal.

"Drapeau seems to be committed to big projects, big federal spending and a the-poor-shall-always-be-with-us mentality," says Toronto's William Kilbourn.

"The Mayor is a great believer in circuses and lotteries," said a city official who asked to remain anonymous. "Maybe that's what we need. In Spain the only thing that keeps people alive is their festivals; their standard of living certainly doesn't."

Drapeau is unimpressed.

"People will always complain," he says. "The city is still in its years of transition. Some areas are still not developed, but they will be. It may be ugly, depressing for a while, but not once we have the money to go ahead and develop those areas."

He claims his primary goal is improving the quality of life in Montreal, regardless of what his political opponents may say. Words like "standard of living" and "humanism" appear frequently in his conversation.

Some of this may have been bending with the political wind in the 1974 election year, but there are signs that the Drapeau-controlled city council is beginning to get a bit tougher with developers. By-law 3411, passed early in 1974, puts tighter limits on building heights and was described by Michael Fish of the Save Montreal group as "a good first step." The move by the Executive Committee in June, 1974, to place tight limits on new construction in the threatened Crescent St. area was another sign that City Hall is beginning to take action.

Part of the reason for the shift in direction was the civic election of November, 1974. People-power city councils with platforms aimed at controlling development had already taken office in Toronto, Vancouver and St. John's, Newfoundland. The growing strength of citizens' groups and preservationist organizations in Montreal and the entry onto the civic scene of parties seeking to take advantage of this situation may have had the Mayor looking over his shoulder.

"What is required is that people of a like mind in municipal government bury their other differences for the sake of achieving an effective coalition," says William Kilbourn.

"Surely people can make an alliance of convenience for the sake of getting Montreal into the housing business, stopping pollution, stopping expressways and controlling development.

"If I were an English-speaking Montrealer interested in this, I would look to form such an alliance of convenience with the trade unions and the Parti Québecois, who are sane, reasonable people. That kind of alliance would be very healthy for Quebec politics—a political force that isn't dominated by the nationalist issue."

Although the Mayor is starting to respond to the challenge, the leadership from City Hall on the direction Montreal's future development should take is still weak and uncertain.

"During the early 1960's, the development of Montreal was masterminded by a skillfull mixture of people, controlled and directed by a happy combination of public and private corporations," says Ray Affleck. "Unfortunately, the same level of good luck and judgment does not exist this time around.

"In the past, Montreal has always developed in a climate of consensus. But now a polarization is taking place, with the developers on one side and the preservationists on the other. The business community is acting as if it had to destroy all the existing values on, for example, Sherbrooke St., in order to create new ones.

"We must get away from this polarization, from childish economic determinism on one side and 100 percent preservation on the other. The city should be taking the lead here, but we are not doing our political homework. We are not getting political leadership in this area."

Planner and urbanist H.P. Daniel van Ginkel agrees: "It's quite obvious what is wrong. It is the whole Montreal climate. The city does not even require developers to publish their plans. That to me, as a European, is absolutely unbelievable.

"In the early 1960's there was a curious ambience in Montreal that made things go right. Businessmen, architects, planners and municipal people were all in general agreement as to which way development should go. That kind of dialogue is missing now."

The provincial government could make some attempt to fill the vacuum by using the 1972 Cultural Property Act for wholesale preservation of buildings of historic or architectural importance, thus forcing changes in development patterns. But so far the Bourassa government has shown little inclination to move in this direction, especially in cases where classifying a building would disrupt a major development program.

"Quebec City doesn't much care about preserving historical things in Montreal," says Judge Kenneth Mackay, a member of the Viger Commission which oversees the protection of Old Montreal. "Neither does the federal government. It has done a lot in Quebec City, but nothing here. Montreal is very low on the federal government's priority list."

Without effective action from one or more levels of government, Montreal's development boom is going to continue its directionless way. The result, says sociologist Kurt Jonassohn, may be to leave people feeling like strangers in their own city.

"The demolition of one house doesn't have much effect," he says. "What does bother people though is the change in the character of a city.

"When every year a house or two is torn down, a street gradually changes from a residential area into another steel canyon.

"All of us have, to some degree, a sense of history. All of us want roots. We like to feel that we belong somewhere, that we are a part of something.

"Somewhere in the world has to feel like home."

Chapter Two

The Saga of the
Van Horne House

The sound of demolition had been heard before in Montreal—the crunching, splintering noises of stone walls and wooden floors falling to wrecking balls. But this time the sound had a special significance.

The solid greystone walls that were being knocked down this time had once been the home of Sir William Cornelius Van Horne, the controversial figure who almost single-handedly built the Canadian Pacific Railroad across Canada almost a century ago.

In the summer of 1973, Van Horne's elegant Victorian mansion on Sherbrooke St. became the center of a controversy that rocked public opinion in Montreal and focused the city's attention for the first time on the architectural wealth that was gradually being destroyed.

On Sept. 7, after a two-month court battle and despite public protests, developer David Azrieli started tearing down the mansion, only hours after receiving a demolition permit. At 9 p.m. on the evening of that day, workmen began removing doors, chandeliers and wood panelling from the building. At 7 a.m. the next morning, the heavy machines moved in and by late afternoon of Sept. 8, Van Horne's house had been reduced to rubble.

Although few Montrealers had ever been inside the mansion, almost everyone who walked or drove along Sherbrooke St. recognized it as a building that characterized the charm and graciousness of another era in the city's history. Perhaps for that reason, hundreds of Montrealers who previously had ignored the demolition of whole blocks of historic houses, gathered on Sherbrooke St. to watch the death throes of the Van Horne mansion.

Some came simply out of curiosity. Others were bitter about what was happening.

An elderly woman stood on the sidewalk, crying. "I remember when that greenhouse was full of flowers," she said, pointing to an ignominious heap of glass and metal.

A station wagon stopped at the curb and a young father stood his daughter on a low stone wall surrounding the site. "I wanted her to see this and remember it," he said.

"This is a disgrace," said another man. "I am ashamed to be a Montrealer."

A woman who lived nearby chided the demolition workers: "Aren't you ashamed of yourselves for tearing down such a beautiful building?" Some of the workmen replied that they didn't agree with what they were doing, but insisted their jobs were at stake. At one point, David Azrieli appeared and said demolition was justified because the plumbing in the house was bad.

While the walls continued to crumble and the dust billowed along Sherbrooke St., some onlookers braved the wrecking balls and police security to save bits and pieces of the house and to grab souvenirs.

Architect Michael Fish dashed in the front door just before the heavy demolition work began and snatched a few pieces of decorative plasterwork—work which had been created decades before by Edward Colonna, one of the founders of Art Nouveau.

Earlier, in the middle of the night, Marianopolis College instructor Victor Garaway managed to sneak into an upper hallway. It was completely panelled in fine wood, he reported later, and

The Van Horne mansion on Sherbrooke Street.
Built 1869, demolished 1973.

lined with bookcases. Only a few hours later the hallway was
flattened, without the panelling being removed.

Some onlookers grabbed stones, bits of damask wall covering,
wrought iron work, pieces of glass—something to keep, something by which to remember what had been an impressive building.

The crowds lingered on until the demolition work was finished.
But one of the people who had tried hardest to save the Van Horne
house was not among the observers. James MacLellan stayed in his
Sherbrooke St. apartment a few blocks away the entire weekend.
He couldn't bear to watch. It was too much like seeing a loved one
tortured to death, he said.

Even after the building was completely demolished and the rubble cleared away, the controversy went on. Outraged letters continued to pour into the offices of *The Star* and *The Gazette*. Petitions seeking to stop further demolition began to be circulated.

The demolition of the Van Horne house had jolted Montrealers. They suddenly recognized a threat to their environment and to the precious balance of old and new which had made the city unique. The euphoria which had been created by the resurgence in the city's economy and the new wave of construction gave way to concern that the city was entering into a process of Manhattanization. Unless the developers were controlled, it was suddenly obvious that within a decade or two Montreal would look like all the other faceless urban centers of North America.

The saga of the Van Horne house had made it clear that neither provincial MNAS nor city councillors intended to interfere with "progress." Efforts to save the building had been rebuffed by government at every turn.

The final chapter in the history of the Van Horne house began in the spring of 1973 when a sharp-eyed architect discovered that an application for a demolition permit on the site had been filed at City Hall on April 18. Through further inquiries, it was learned that developer David Azrieli had taken an option on the property and was planning to build a high-rise office tower on the site.

Surviving members of the Van Horne family revealed they had been trying to sell the mansion for several years. It had become a greystone elephant, impossible to maintain because it stood on prime development land at the corner of Sherbrooke and Stanley streets. The site was evaluated at $50.00 a square foot. Yearly taxes on the property had reached $31,000.

Azrieli's offer to buy the house was conditional on obtaining permission to demolish it. His option had been taken out months before, but it was only in June, 1973, that it was made public. At first, the buyer refused to be identified.

When the first reports of the building's impending demise were made public, there was some alarm but no action. The Canadian Pacific Ltd., for instance, refused to intervene despite Van Horne's historic connection with the company.

Then, at the end of June, one Montrealer got upset enough about the situation to do something about saving the house. Ironically, he turned out to be an employee of CP Ltd.—a young marketing executive named James MacLellan. He had had several apartment buildings demolished from underneath him, and he felt the Van Horne house shouldn't meet the same fate. In an attempt to stop the developer's plans, MacLellan went to court in an unprecedented class action bid to prevent the house's demolition.

MacLellan had learned that the house had been proposed months earlier for historic classification—a prerogative of the Quebec Minister of Cultural Affairs which, if approval was given, would save the building. The minister at the time, Dr. François Cloutier, had already announced his intention to proceed with classification under the terms of the 1972 Cultural Property Act.

On May 8, 1973, the Department of Cultural Affairs officially notified Royal Trust Co., trustee of the Van Horne estate, of the minister's intention to classify the property. But on June 14, the department wrote again to the company to state that it had been decided that no such action would be taken. No reason was given for the change in plans.

When the government's decision became known, MacLellan wrote to Dr. Cloutier to ask that he reconsider placing the mansion under provincial government protection. On the basis of that request, MacLellan applied for an interlocutory injunction to prevent the building's destruction until the minister could render a final decision.

MacLellan also said in his petition to the court that removal of the Van Horne mansion from its corner site would damage the ·charm and atmosphere of the neighborhood (he lived just a short distance away) and would destroy valuable green space. He also claimed that further high-rise development along Sherbrooke St. would increase traffic congestion, escalate property values in the area, mar the view of Mount Royal, and strain social services.

It was a unique situation: an ordinary citizen going to court to claim that his right to peaceful enjoyment of the environment should be given legal precedence over a private individual's right to dispose of his own property as he saw fit. The case created an immediate sensation in the Montreal press.

To aid his fight to save the mansion, MacLellan hurriedly formed an organization called Great Places which campaigned publicly on behalf of the Van Horne house and other threatened buildings.

Round one went to Azrieli. MacLellan's petition was denied by the court. But his lawyer, E. Michael Berger, immediately filed an appeal, thereby keeping the case alive.

There followed nearly two months of court battles, public campaigns and representations to various levels of government in a desperate attempt to save the house. The battle at times took on the flavor and drama of a best-selling novel, full of secret dealings, political manoeuverings and courtroom confrontations. In the end, MacLellan lost. But what transpired between July 10 and September 7 opened the eyes of Montrealers to the forces that were at work in the city.

It also marked the first time in Montreal's history that a member of the general public had been strongly enough concerned about the city's cultural heritage to fight for it in a court of law.

There was a great deal of sympathy for MacLellan's battle inside City Hall. Officials in the city planning department were eager to see the mansion saved, as were a number of city councillors. But the city was hampered by the restrictions of its charter and had no power to intervene. Under the law as it now stands, Montreal does not have the authority to refuse to grant a demolition permit if all legal requirements are met and the developer is acting within zoning regulations.

An amendment to the City Charter would be required to change this situation. Given the law as it stood in the summer of 1973, all city authorities could do was to refuse to issue a demolition permit as long as the case was before the courts. There was even some question as to whether Montreal's power went that far. Normally, demolition permits are issued when applied for and there have been suggestions that the city was acting illegally in withholding a permit from Azrieli, court case or no court case. Leo Laurin, director of the Permits Departments, was not at all happy with the situation.

While the city, legally or illegally, was doing what it could to hold up demolition, however, the provincial government was doing everything in its power to get the building demolished. The Minister of Cultural Affairs, who in May had felt the house important enough to classify, turned his back on the situation. Appeals to Premier Robert Bourassa to intervene fell on deaf ears. It was suggested long after the house was demolished that the switch in provincial government attitudes was in large part due to the intervention of former Quebec Premier Jean Lesage, who remains a behind-the-scenes force in the Liberal Party and who was retained as legal counsel in the dispute. But, none of the principals in the dispute have ever confirmed the extent of Lesage's role.

There were certainly forces of some sort at work in the background, however, because in refusing to proceed with classification of the house Dr. Cloutier was acting against the advice of his most knowledgeable advisers.

The Cultural Property Commission, which was set up in 1972 to advise the minister on precisely such issues, had strongly recommended that the house be classified and protected. So had the Viger Commission, the body set up to oversee the preservation of Old Montreal.

When Dr. Cloutier ignored the advice of his own Cultural Property Commission, its members objected strongly. In a July 10 telegram to Premier Bourassa, they said the minister had acted contrary to their advice and demanded that the Van Horne mansion be classified immediately. Bourassa, who was acting Minister of Cultural Affairs while Cloutier was on holiday, claimed he never received the telegram.

Growing public demands for an explanation as to why the government was not acting brought a strange reply from Marcel Junius, Director General of National Cultural Property. He said the minister had refused to classify the mansion because it was not "typically Québecois." He also engaged in a bit of buck-passing, saying the province had no money to aid in the preservation or restoration of old buildings, even though such powers had been specifically set out in the 1972 law. He suggested help to save the building should come from the federal government.

The only federal organization which might have been in a position to help was the National Historic Sites and Monuments Board. But it had not been asked to classify the mansion and even if it had been, it did not have the power to save the building from demolition.

Unlike the Quebec Cultural Property Act, federal laws dealing with historic preservation do not protect classified property. Unless the federal government buys a building outright or in cooperation with a public or private group, its powers are restricted to designating a building as being of historic importance and affixing a plaque to it. No plaque has ever been known to stop a wrecker's ball. In the case of the Van Horne house, the federal government also maintained it had no authority to interfere with the disposal of private property. This threw the onus right back on Quebec City.

Quebec's reaction continued to be negative. At one point there was a suggestion that the provincial government would reconsider classification. But the Minister of Cultural Affairs effectively dragged his heels until only hours before demolition was set to begin. By then, it was too late.

While the three levels of government were passing the buck, public indignation grew. During the hot months of July and August, the controversy raged in the newspapers and on radio and television stations.

Some Montrealers felt the building should be saved at any cost. Others said it should be destroyed. The suggestion was even made that the sooner it be demolished, the better because the CPR and Van Horne had used Chinese coolies and "slave labor" to build their railway. Presumably knocking down his house would somehow erase this segment of Canadian history.

There were suggestions that the Montreal Museum of Fine Arts should buy the mansion. Museum director David G. Carter was one of those anxious to save the house, but he insisted later, in defending the museum's refusal to move, that the building did not lend itself well to conversion into an annex and that undertaking the cost of maintaining the house could have put the museum in serious financial difficulty.

Other logical purchasers of the house found similar reasons for backing away.

Meanwhile, debate grew over the real architectural value of the building. Some experts claimed the mansion was unique, with an interior that had been in part created by Edward Colonna, the Belgian-born protegé of Louis Tiffany and Samuel Bing and one of the founders of Art Nouveau.

Dr. Martin Eidelberg, a professor of art at Rutgers University in New Jersey, declared the Van Horne mansion to be the only complete example of Colonna's work in North America. The ornamental plaster and gilt work was considered to be extremely fine. Only bits and pieces of this type of Colonna work survive, scattered in museums throughout the world. The Van Horne mansion contained an entire room of it.

David Azrieli was unimpressed. He contended the Colonna work was ugly, and hired several architects to go through the house.

"They found nothing worth saving," he declared.

One of his architects, however, said later that, while the building was a jumble of different styles, it was typically Victorian and should be saved to preserve the character of Sherbrooke St.

"It has merit from a town planning point of view," said Edouard Fiset, a well-respected Montreal architect.

Azrieli did not ask any historians to evaluate the house. He said he didn't think it was historically valuable.

Some Montrealers agreed with him. Others didn't, but contended the house wasn't worth saving because it was an architectural bastard.

James MacLellan and Great Places argued that the house was both historically and architecturally significant. They also stressed the importance of Colonna's work in a 200-page brief which they hurriedly assembled for submission to the Minister of Cultural Affairs.

Representatives of the department promised to reconsider the situation if the document was "significant." Later, the government said it might consider classifying Colonna's work and moving it to a museum—a somewhat precarious idea since the work was all of plaster of Paris.

In the end, the province did nothing. In a classic example of the government's attitude, the Department of Cultural Affairs sent representatives to examine the house at the eleventh hour, one day before the final September 7 court hearing at which Azrieli was granted his demolition permit. The experts viewed the building and returned to Quebec City to prepare their report. It was handed to Dr. Cloutier after the Van Horne house was rubble. It recommended that the building be saved.

Throughout the entire controversy, Azrieli, Royal Trust and Van Horne executor, lawyer Matthew Hannon refused to allow anyone to tour the mansion. Reporters and photographers were banned, said Hannon, because "I prefer unbiased reporting." How the press was supposed to be unbiased without ever viewing the interior of the building was never explained.

A plea from one Montrealer who wanted to buy the house and preserve it fell on deaf ears. Phyllis Bronfman Lambert, an architect and a member of the wealthy Bronfman family, said she was willing to pay more than the $800,000 asking price. Her idea was to turn the mansion into headquarters for Cemp, a family-run investment company. But she was never allowed to inspect the mansion to see if such a venture were possible, nor was she permitted to bid on the house. When she finally did get to see the interior on the last night before the house was demolished, she described it as "extremely beautiful."

The 52-room mansion had been built in 1869 by John Hamilton. Van Horne purchased it in 1889, when he was starting work for the CPR. His family continued to live there through most of the 20th century, surrounded by servants, luxury and Van Horne's magnificent art collection. It wasn't until 1967 that the widow of Van Horne's grandson moved out. She had been selling off the art and book collections, and the mansion itself no longer interested her or other surviving members of the family. Nor did the family seem particularly interested in having the building preserved; no request from the Van Hornes was ever made to the provincial government to classify the house.

The family's seeming indifference to the fate of the house and the provincial government's steadfast refusal to intervene sealed the fate of the building. When the courts turned down MacLellan's petition, Azrieli was free to move in his wrecking crews. He lost no time in doing so.

The destruction of the Van Horne house was a loss to Montreal, the Province of Quebec and Canada as a whole. The mansion had stood for decades as a visible reminder of one of the larger-than-life figures who had built the nation. In the space of less than 24 hours, a developer reduced it to a pile of shattered masonry and twisted steel.

Chapter Three

The Edifice Complex

For a century, Montreal was a city famed for its old-world charm. It was a green and pleasant town with tree-lined streets, mansions along the boulevards, rows of attractive brick and greystone houses, elegant churches and tranquil parks.

But that Montreal is rapidly disappearing. Clusters of high-rise apartments are replacing the unique greystones. The central core is being turned into a labyrinth of parking lots and office towers. Older buildings are being allowed to fall into disrepair and decay.

Graceful Montreal is becoming indistinguishable from any other ill-planned North American metropolis. Random development is turning it into an urban sea of concrete and glass.

Some of the old charm still remains. But relentless development and political apathy are combining to destroy Montreal's unique flavor as the Paris of North America.

Montreal has acquired an international reputation as a wide-open city for developers. That term was actually used to describe the town at a builders' convention in Detroit in 1973.

Investment money, both domestic and international, began flowing into the city in the early 1970's, after the political climate stabilized following the October crisis of 1970. The flow of cash increased in 1973 and 1974, partly because of events in other Canadian cities.

Vancouver and Toronto both experienced major building booms. But people-power reactions in both cities brought sweeping changes in municipal government which led directly to tighter controls on developers. Toronto became even less attractive to development money when new legislation came into force in Ontario in the spring of 1974 which slapped a 20 percent transfer tax on the sale of property to non-Canadians.

But in Montreal, which had been starved for new investment since the halcyon days leading up to Expo 67, the climate remained warm and welcoming despite murmurs of discontent from a few environmental groups. Developers began to look upon the city as a sort of Canadian banana republic, welcoming their cash with open arms and placing few restrictions on how they spent it. They responded accordingly.

A Toronto real-estate agent acting on behalf of three West German banks commented: "Investments in Ontario have become unattractive, if not absolutely out of the question." His clients are now concentrating on the Prairie provinces and Quebec, and looking at Montreal in particular.

The reason for Montreal's attractiveness isn't hard to find. The city badly needs increased taxation revenues from new development in the downtown area. Home-owners in Montreal are already among the highest-taxed in Canada and the city can no longer count on raising their mill rates to meet escalating costs. The only solution is more industry and more large-scale mid-town construction. The Drapeau-dominated city council has been willing to tolerate major changes in the face of the city in order to achieve these ends and get more cash flowing into the municipal treasury.

Explains Richard Glickman: "It's a question of getting the best and highest use out of the land. That's why the mayor likes what is happening. A city has to operate within a budget, and it gets its money from taxes. It's to the city's advantage to have high-rises, to increase land values, to get more taxes."

Highrise construction on Simpson Street
between Sherbrooke Street and McGregor Avenue

Adds developer Vincent Ponte: "If you suppress development in the core area, taxes have to go up for home-owners, because this is the goose that lays the golden egg. Canadian Pacific's proposed redevelopment plans would generate about $6 million a year alone in new tax revenue for the city."

Montreal's property tax system works in favor of this kind of development. All property is taxed at a standard mill rate based on an evaluation which is usually about 90 percent of market value. The evaluation includes the value of both land and buildings.

Thus if a person owns a low-rise building and a high-rise goes up next door, the market value of his property increases. So, obviously, do his taxes.

The tax disincentive to maintain older buildings in the downtown area is further increased by the federal corporate tax structure which allows companies to write off depreciation on new buildings but requires payment of recaptured depreciation if an older building is eventually sold at a profit.

Says Glickman, with a great deal of truth: "There's no way a three or four-storey building can survive downtown."

No way, that is, unless the tax system is revised or politicians take action to preserve a specific area. There were signs in the summer of 1974 that might be starting to happen. Montreal city council, apparently stung by growing public criticism of the carnage in the city center and facing an autumn civic election, introduced measures to protect the Crescent St. area against large-scale development.

The council's actions appeared to effectively protect this unique corner of Montreal against further encroachments and was the first real indication that City Hall might be prepared to start pulling in the welcome mat for developers. But preservationist groups were quick to point out that the action was only a first step and that much still remains to be done. As Michael Fish put it: "This will only shunt problems from one area to another and a lot of good housing will go down the drain in the meantime. I'm not going to be bought off by 10 city blocks when 110 need attention."

City council's reluctance to interfere in private development projects is one cause for concern among environmental groups. Another is the almost total lack of city-imposed building and architectural standards. Developers have carte blanche to throw up shoddily-built high-rises.

The planned obsolescence which characterizes the latest wave of Montreal construction results directly from this lack of control.

The economics of high-rise apartment construction result in a property being paid off and returning its maximum profit in about 30 years, sometimes less. That means buildings are constructed to last just about that long. Montreal's weak building code permits the cheap construction methods that make this possible. For quick-buck developers, that means maximum profits.

Apart from weak regulations governing the structure of a building, the city also exercises no control over the architectural style of new buildings. No effort is made to ensure they will harmonize with surrounding structures. Nor are rigid safety standards applied—there is no law, for instance, requiring builders to equip high-rises with sprinkler systems.

This laissez-faire attitude on the part of City Hall has played a large part in attracting development money into the city.

Comments Judge Kenneth Mackay, a member of the Viger Commission: "Those guys sitting in West Germany, what do they care? If the city doesn't demand any architectural standards, why not do it as cheaply as possible?"

Many of the development firms which are most active in Montreal are based in Europe. Others are heavily backed by foreign capital, and so tend to put a higher priority on obtaining a large return on investment than on attempting to preserve local traditions or history. Still others are controlled by men who came to Canada from abroad and who lack the basic background necessary to understand Canadian values.

David Azrieli is one example. He built duplexes in Ville d'Anjou and high-rises in Cote St. Luc and Milton-Park before tackling the biggest project of his life—an office tower on fashionable Sherbrooke St. on the site of the Van Horne house.

Azrieli described himself once in a newspaper interview as being from Israel. When asked about his views on the historical value of the Van Horne mansion when the fight was raging to save it, he told a journalist: "It's just a house. And anyway, this man Van Horne was born in the U.S."

Ian Martin, a native of Australia, is an architect who has advanced plans for several projects that would have changed the face of the city. One of his proposals involves the former Soeurs de Bon Pasteur property on Sherbrooke St., which backs onto the gracious elegance of St. Louis Square.

Martin prepared the project with fellow architect Russell Edge, designer of McGill University's often criticised Samuel Bronfman building. They received financial backing from Swiss Procan Finanz AG to erect two 23-storey towers on the site.

Local citizens immediately protested that the plan would block sunlight from St. Louis Square and would greatly increase traffic in the area. Their complaints were heard at City Hall, which moved to block the project, at least temporarily.

Martin was also involved in a project which would have resulted in the demolition of the Shaughnessy house on Dorchester Blvd. West, which has since been classified as an historic monument by the provincial government.

When his plans for the site were rejected in favor of a scheme put forward by the Toronto firm of Y & R Properties, which provided for the preservation and restoration of the house, Martin filed suit against the former owners, the Sisters of Service. His suit, which is still before the courts, claims over $600,000 for, among other things, the legal costs in fighting classification and "loss of profits."

Marcel Elefant's family was already wealthy when they left North Africa to settle in Canada. Elefant has added to the family fortunes as a successful developer in the downtown area. He has built buildings like the shiny black tower at Bleury and St. Catherine St., and recently has been assembling property on Sherbrooke St. between St. Matthew and St. Mark, paying close to $100,000 for each building. He has already revealed plans for a high-rise on the site, but so far the project appears to have stalled.

Famous Players, the movie theatre chain owned by Paramount Pictures, which is in turn owned by the giant U.S. conglomerate Gulf & Western, controls the majority of cinemas in Montreal. These include many of the fine old movie palaces built between 1910 and 1930.

With movie attendance at the downtown theatres declining, Famous Players finds itself in possession of vast areas of prime development property. In 1973, it demolished the venerable (1921) Capitol Theatre, the most magnificent movie palace ever built in the city. It is currently replacing it with an office tower which will bear the name Le Centre Capitol. The company is also reported to have plans for other downtown theatres, including the Palace which was Canada's first sound movie house and which was opulently decorated by the great theatre interior designer Emmanuel Briffa.

Yale Properties is a giant firm, with property investments in Montreal estimated at around $50 million. It is controlled by the seven Iranian-born Mashaal brothers. In early 1974, the company acquired two of Montreal's most distinguished residential buildings: the Bishop Court Apartments on Bishop St. and a row of greystones on Baile St. which were built as guest-houses by Lord Strathcona, and in which Dr. Norman Bethune lived during the 1930's. Acquisition of these buildings by the firm immediately raised fears that an attempt would be made to demolish them and to redevelop the sites.

Yale is one of the biggest development firms in Montreal, with interests everywhere. It controls a bewildering series of subsidiary companies, and seems to create a new one for every separate property transaction it gets involved in. Curzon Properties, controlled by Yale, bought the Bishop Court building. Perfort, controlled by Yale, bought the houses on Baile St. In addition, Yale controls Tricon Construction, St. James Holding Corporation, Nationwide Capital Ltd., and other firms.

Salim Mashaal, one of the brothers who control Yale, strongly objects to the "bad guys" image which he claims newspapers have given developers. He blames the city's tax structure for making it unprofitable to preserve low-rise buildings.

Trizec is the biggest of the foreign-controlled companies operating in Montreal. Founded out of the ashes of William Zeckendorf's Place Ville Marie venture, the firm controls over $600 million worth of Canadian real estate. Trizec is British-controlled—66 percent of the company is in the hands of Star Holdings Inc.

The company has been steadily expanding and within the past few years has acquired Cummings Properties and Great West International Equities, both based in Calgary; these were Canada's fifth and seventh largest development firms, respectively, until Trizec took them over. Through interlocking directorships, it has links with most of Canada's major financial houses including the Bank of Nova Scotia, the Royal Bank of Canada, Sun Life, Canadian Pacific Investments, and Greenshields. Since these companies all tend to invest heavily in real estate, the links are important.

In Montreal, Trizec owns Place Ville Marie, the Royal Bank Building on St. James St., the Banque Canadienne Nationale Building on Place d'Armes, the Drummond Medical Building, the Peel Center Building and the Sherbrooke Apartments. It also manages Place Bonaventure.

Trizec is not known for being particularly responsive to public opinion when its development activities come under scrutiny. One official of the firm has even suggested that "private interest groups are often behind the promotion of saving buildings." The company will not commit itself to the permanent preservation of any of its buildings because, in the words of a spokesman, "it wouldn't be fair to our successors."

The company likes to point to the preservation of the Loyalist House in Saint John, New Brunswick, as an example of its "corporate spirit." What its spokesmen often forget to add is the fact that the house was designated as a building of national historic significance in 1959 and was restored by federal funds and opened as a museum in 1965.

After Trizec, Canada's second-biggest real-estate company is the Toronto-based Cadillac-Fairview Corporation. It is controlled by Cemp Investments Ltd. of Montreal which is owned by the children of Samuel Bronfman.

Cadillac-Fairview came into being on May 31, 1974, as the result of a merger of Cadillac Development Corporation, Fairview Corporation and Canadian Equity and Development. The company has assets in excess of $600 million. Its main interests in the Montreal area are in suburban shopping centers, which were built by Fairview, but it also owns the Dominion Square Building.

The links between Cemp and Trizec are worthy of note. Two Bronfmans, cousins of the Cemp Bronfmans, sit on the board of Trizec. Phillip F. Vineberg is a director of Cadillac-Fairview while his law firm, Phillips & Vineberg, handles the affairs of Trizec and Cemp. His partner, Lazarus Phillips, is a director of both Trizec and Cemp. Cadillac-Fairview chairman A.E. Diamond is on the board of Eagle Star Insurance Co. of Canada, controlled by Star Holdings Inc. of England which also controls Trizec. There are many other connections between these two companies, which are alleged to be competitors.

Montreal has a number of relatively small-time builders who specialize in high-rise apartments in areas like Lincoln Ave. Central Holdings, owned by the Zentner family of Hampstead, is one such company. It has built, among other things, the Chateau Latour on de Maisonneuve St. at St. Matthew and a new high-rise one block to the east. Both are reinforced concrete towers.

These buildings are often sold immediately on completion, frequently to Europeans who hold them as investment properties pending the day when a better and higher use for the land can be found.

"You don't make money owning a building," says Glickman of Central Holdings. "Taxes hit you, and the new lease laws. The money you make is in selling the building once it is built, often to buyers from Germany, these days. They buy them on future profits."

Whether they are building high-rise apartments or office towers and whether their intention is to sell the building or manage it, developers have one thing in common : they thrive on secrecy. Old buildings can be demolished, new foundations laid and structures begin to rise without the public being given any idea what is going on. Signs identifying a high-rise development are rare, and the companies in charge of the projects are often fronts for other firms.

Some of the development firms carry this obsession with secrecy right into their own corporate structure.

Gipala Properties is an example. Run by Israelis and reportedly financed by Italian capital, the company recently bought the Royal George Apartments, with its magnificent facade. It is also involved in a massive plan for the redevelopment of the Berkeley Hotel site, which reportedly will cost $30 million.

Gipala and two of its officers who have been identified, Gilbert Zemour and Alain Checroune, maintain the tightest possible secrecy about their plans. They simply refuse to discuss them.

Gipala was incorporated in Quebec on February 25, 1974, by three "provisional applicants for charter." The three are Daniel Morris, Georgette Lavoie and Sheila Kashner. Morris is a lawyer from the Montreal firm of Morris & Kravitz. Lavoie is one of the firm's employees. Kashner is an employee of the accounting firm of

Sorkin & Richer which, like Morris & Kravitz, has offices at 625 Dorchester Blvd. West. The three declined to name the parties for whom they were acting in incorporating Gipala Properties.

But development in Montreal isn't confined to foreign-owned firms or to companies with undetermined origins. Some of the biggest public companies in Canada are also involved.

The giant, Ottawa-based Campeau Corporation unveiled plans in 1973 for a massive redevelopment project for the land around Blue Bonnets raceway in the north end of the city. The plan includes two 75-storey towers. Neighboring municipalities such as the Town of Mount Royal have tried without success to obtain more details about the project. There is concern about the problems of traffic flow and the supplying of services to a massive development of this type, but so far Campeau hasn't provided answers.

Complexe Desjardins, one of the biggest projects currently underway in Montreal, is financed by the Caisses Populaire Desjardins group. The method used to get it started is not untypical of the way things are done in this city: the land needed for the project was expropriated by the City of Montreal and then leased back to the company for 60 years. The group expects to have its investment returned in 40 years.

Canadian Pacific is another firm that is getting into the development business in Montreal. There is an irony in this: this bedrock Canadian firm which has played such an important role in the historical development of the country was responsible for the threat to one of mid-town Montreal's most architecturally significant buildings, Windsor Station.

Like movie theatre companies, CP Ltd. has found itself with a great deal of excess land in the center of Montreal as a result of the decline in railroad traffic. For some time, the company has been studying plans for the redevelopment of its 15-acre site around Windsor Station.

During the late 1960's and early 1970's , various plans were unveiled, promoted and then quietly dropped. All of them tended to regard Windsor Station as a disposable item, despite its obvious architectural and historical value. So determined was the company to get rid of the building, that it even went so far as to tear up the tracks leading to the platforms in preparation for demolition. The work was stopped at that point, but for more than two years CP passengers arriving at Windsor Station have had to trudge half a mile through snow and rain before reaching cover because of the company's haste in relocating the railhead.

When opposition to the demolition of the station began to grow, CP took the project out of the hands of its real-estate subsidiary, Marathon Realties Ltd. The New York firm of James D. Landauer Associates was hired to do a feasibility study of the site. It came up with a 70-page report containing advice such as: "It is important that CP be cognizant of the French-Canadian presence in Montreal. It also advised CP to retain Windsor Station: "It is obvious that the issue of Windsor Station's development is the most significant question around which community groups could mobilize opposition to the proposed development." It suggested further that CP build up to 10 buildings of varying heights on the site.

The contract for designing the complex has gone to the enormous, prestigious American architectural firm of Skidmore, Owings & Merill, after an unconvincing contest between it and two relatively minor Toronto firms for the job.

There now appears a good chance that Windsor Station will survive as a luxury apartment hotel. But it is troublesome that a company with a history so closely entwined with Canada's should have given serious consideration for so long to demolishing it.

Although CP is not a crown corporation, many Canadians tend to regard it as a public institution. As a result, they expect more from it in the way of setting examples for other firms. But the performance of public institutions in Montreal in preserving the character of the city has been less than encouraging.

The Montreal General Hospital is still criticized for building squarely between the mountain and the city. The universities have been indifferent developers at best: Sir George Williams University (now part of Concordia University) gave the downtown area a distinctly unattractive building and now is studying plans for expansion along Bishop and Mackay, an area of Victorian greystones and red sandstones; the University of Montreal has been busy erecting a string of high-rises on the north slope of the mountain. McGill University has knocked down some of the city's finest old homes for its expansion projects.

Governments haven't done much better. The provincial government imposed a number of buildings of questionable architectural value on Montreal, including the Quebec Police Force building on Parthenais St. and the new Court House, an aggressively modern structure directly across the street from the 18th and 19th century buildings of Old Montreal. The Quebec government is also responsible for the destruction of the magnificent St. Jacques Church at the corner of St. Catherine and St. Denis Streets for the campus of the University of Quebec, and for the Trans-Canada autoroute which was gouged out across the face of Montreal at the cost of 3,000 homes.

The federal government's contributions have been to destroy an established residential area in the city's east end in order to build Maison de Radio-Canada, and to wipe out a good part of Chinatown to make way for Place Guy Favreau.

So far, there has been very little protest against this type of development from establishment circles in Montreal. The Montreal Real Estate Board, for instance, seems to welcome it. Commented its president, Johan Draper of Canada Permanent Trust: "Sure they're beautiful houses. Take a picture of them and tear them down."

Chapter Four

Visions of the Future

A current of excitement runs through the exclusive Beaver Club in the Queen Elizabeth Hotel at lunchtime. There's a sense of power, an atmosphere of big money, a feeling of important plans being made as some of Montreal's most influential people cut into their chateaubriand. They speak in hushed tones of banks and new buildings, of the stock market, of governments, of millions of dollars in bond issues. Cabinet ministers dine with lawyers, business executives meet brokers. There is a feeling of important things happening, of decisions being made between sips of 1966 Chambertin that will affect the lives of thousands of people.

The maître d' bows. Headwaiters appear. "Good afternoon, Mr. Ponte. Here's your table, Mr. Ponte. A martini, sir, dry, just the way you like them. We have Boston Bibb lettuce today, Mr. Ponte, your favorite."

There's time for a horse-racing story before yet another waiter appears, bringing a telephone message. Then the slight, Italian-looking man in dark glasses settles back and talks about one of his favorite subjects: Montreal.

Vincent de Pasciuoto-Ponte likes Beaver Club martinis, Boston Bibb lettuce and Rodin lithographs. And he loves Montreal with a

The plaza at Place Ville Marie

passion. A Boston-educated urban planner, he is one of the city's biggest boosters. He travels thousands of miles every year, telling the world what Montreal has to offer and encouraging businessmen in other countries to invest their money in the city.

Ponte is a logical person to sell Montreal, for he knows more about the city's development than most other people. It was his concept of a multi-level city within a city that helped spark one of the biggest building booms in Montreal's history.

The idea wasn't new, as Ponte himself is quick to point out. In fact, it is 500 years old. Leonardo da Vinci invented the concept of cities operating on several levels and his sketches and drawings depicting layered transportation systems can still be seen in the Vatican museum.

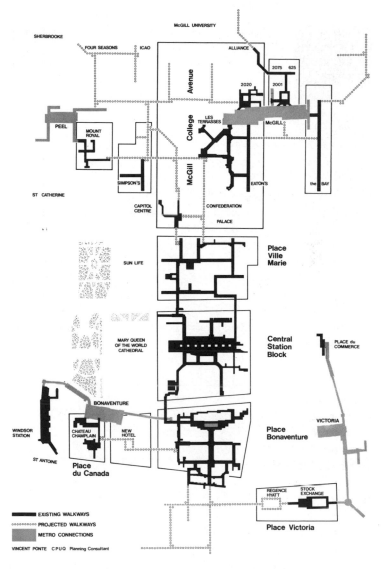

Pedestrian network in downtown Montreal

Nor was the building boom of the early 1960's, which brought the multi-level city to Montreal, the first of its kind here. The mid-19th century was a tremendous period of construction in the city. The turn of the century saw another building boom, producing many of the stone structures now threatened by redevelopment. Yet another construction boom occurred after the Second World War during the great rush to provide housing for veterans.

But nothing compares with the development renaissance that started in Montreal in the late 1950's and carried on until Expo 67.

It began with a 22-acre hole in the ground next to Dorchester Blvd., right in the heart of the city. The hole, as it was unaffectionately known by Montrealers for decades, contained the tracks of the Canadian National Railway's northern commuter route, which disappeared under Mount Royal. There had been talk of developing the eyesore for years, but nothing was done until the 1950's. Then, through the initiative of Donald Gordon, then president of the CNR, top officials of the Royal Bank of Canada and Mayor Jean Drapeau, all that changed. Developer William Zeckendorf was brought to Montreal and he, along with Ponte and architect I.M. Pei, turned the hole into the Queen Elizabeth Hotel and Place Ville Marie.

PVM became the first phase in what tourist brochures now promote as "Montreal's underground city." In fact, some of the "underground city" is really above the surface because of the way the land slopes towards the river. "Sheltered city" is a more accurate term to describe what the developers began to create when they hit on the idea of turning PVM's basement into a shopping mall.

The opening of Place Ville Marie in 1962 became the central event in the development boom that completely changed the face of central Montreal during the 1960's. Numerous other major buildings followed in rapid succession, along with the Metro and Expo 67. The wave of new construction boosted the city's annual tax revenues by millions of dollars.

While the face of the city changed above ground, the sheltered city grew too. Reaching out tentacles like a concrete octopus, it extended southward from Place Ville Marie, through Central Station and into Place Bonaventure. To the west, the sheltered city stretched out to embrace the new Chateau Champlain Hotel and Windsor Station.

There it halted temporarily, but now it is beginning to grow again. By 1985, Ponte predicts that Montreal will have almost seven miles of sheltered pedestrian walkways in the downtown area, creating an urban complex unique in the world.

Most of the major commercial buildings currently under construction in the mid-town area will eventually be plugged in. Although they appear to the casual viewer to be springing up like so many mushrooms in a damp cellar, Ponte and developers like him claim there is a reason why so much construction is taking place at the same time within such a small area of the city. They are part of the closest thing downtown Montreal has to a master plan for the future. They constitute what amounts to a grand design for the expansion of the sheltered city concept.

This doesn't mean that all the construction taking place in central Montreal is desirable, however. Although some of the new buildings have been well planned and imaginatively conceived, others will add little to the aesthetic value of the city core. Nor will all of the towers currently springing up be plugged in to the sheltered city.

There is a major difference between the way development is taking place now and the way it all began more than a decade ago.

"In the beginning, it was done by one developer, the CNR," Ponte says. "Now it is all being done piecemeal, by individual developers. They are each inserting their own pedestrian systems, on their own initiative, with private money and without intervention."

In spite of this piecemeal approach, Ponte sees the sheltered pedestrian network extending from below St. Antoine St. to above Sherbrooke within 10 years.

49

He sees the evolution taking place through the formation of a new unit of the sheltered city north of St. Catherine St., centered on McGill College Ave. At the same time, the existing system will expand south to include Place Victoria and new developments planned for the St. Antoine—St. James St. area. Eventually, the two sections will be hooked up through a passage under St. Catherine St.

All this explains why the area around McGill College Ave. has suddenly become the construction center of Montreal. Original plans for the district called for identical buildings on either side of the avenue, with covered pedestrian arcades at street level. Planners saw it as a North American version of the Rue de Rivoli in Paris.

But these ideas were scrapped, for various reasons, and were replaced by something less grandiose. The street will be widened into a boulevard, but it will not be developed in the coordinated way the planners had originally hoped.

The first stage of the McGill College Ave. development will be the Centre Capitol, which will rise on the site of the demolished Capitol Theatre. Eaton's Les Terrasses, a shopping and office complex, will follow right behind. These two developments will form the core of the new unit of the sheltered city.

Also plugged into the new system will be the major buildings at 2001, 2020 and 2075 University, 625 President Kennedy, the new Alliance Insurance Building at 680 Sherbrooke West, and the planned Maisonneuve Hotel at the Maisonneuve and McGill College Ave.

Plans for the area west of McGill College, between St. Catherine and Sherbrooke, are still being studied. Eventually, however, the pedestrian system will be extended to include Simpson's, the Mount Royal Hotel and the Peel Metro stop.

It is likely, but not definite, that walkways will also connect new developments currently going up on Sherbrooke between Peel and Mansfield: the Four Seasons Hotel and the International Civil

Aviation Organization Building. Other office and apartment complexes which will rise on lots that are now vacant will probably be plugged in too.

McGill University has future plans to construct a passageway from the Alliance Insurance Building to its campus, where most buildings are already linked by tunnels. That will plug the whole McGill complex into the sheltered city. Along St. Catherine St., two to three miles of sheltered pedestrian walks will link the city's three main department stores: Simpsons, Eaton's and The Bay. The entire northern section will be linked to Place Ville Marie when the Confederation Building and the Palace Theatre on St. Catherine St. are torn down and redeveloped, which Ponte says must happen.

To the south, the sheltered city will expand between Place Bonaventure and the Chateau Champlain to include the 40-storey Hotel Concordia, which is to be built on the parking lot directly behind Mary Queen of the World Cathedral. To the east of Place Bonaventure, pedestrian walkways will link up with Place Victoria, including the Montreal Stock Exchange and a second tower in the complex, now being constructed.

Ponte sees all this as using Montreal's small, 200-acre central core to the best possible advantage. To do this, he says, development must be compressed and built upwards, downwards and sideways. It must be multi-level and serve a variety of purposes: transportation, commercial and residential.

When Place Ville Marie first opened, merchants were reluctant to rent space in its 175,000-square foot pedestrian mall. Underground stores had never been tried in Montreal before; retailers were afraid that, without shop windows facing onto the street, customers would stay away in droves. The success story of the underground mall astonished them; now it is almost impossible to get space.

People liked the sheltered city concept. They enjoyed not having to walk in the rain or to trudge through cold and snow in mid-winter to shop. They liked the idea of being able to go directly from their offices to a restaurant and then do some shopping without ever putting on a coat. The attraction of the sheltered shops and boutiques is highlighted by one statistic: every day approximately 90,000 people walk through the shop-lined promenades leading from Central Station to the PVM offices. Only 10,000 take the shorter, duller route at the other end of the station, which leads through a plain, tiled corridor. The walkway system is not perfect—it lacks washrooms, coat-check rooms and tends to be overheated. But people love it.

The underground complex also has the advantage of separating people from their cars. As more walkways are added, it will become increasingly easy to use the Metro and to have access to the entire downtown area through the sheltered city route. Centrally located underground parking areas encourage people to drive into town, then park their cars and leave them for the day. This helps relieve traffic congestion, as do the sheltered trucking routes pioneered in buildings like Place Bonaventure.

The imagination that has gone into the development of the sheltered city has stimulated other innovative designs in the city center. Les Terrasses, which will be built between Eaton's and Kresge's is an example.

The $20 million project, first of its kind in North America, will be built on a series of split-level terraces, designed to make the pedestrian feel like he is floating. Glass will replace concrete wherever possible and entrance to the complex will be through an "air curtain" rather than through a door.

Stores in the complex will be serviced by a series of interior truck ramps. Below ground, the complex will be part of the expansion of the CNR tracks, providing new links with suburban centers and with the Mirabel jetport. On the roof there will be a garden, the first of its kind in the city.

Les Terrasses promises to be the kind of development Montreal needs—an imaginative project which does not involve the destruction of a community or a valuable building.

Three other projects now underway are also trying to be imaginative and different—but are not succeeding to anything like the same extent, partly because they have all chosen the same "innovation:" a covering of bronze reflecting glass.

Two of the buildings are directly across from each other, on opposite sides of Sherbrooke St. at the corner of Stanley. Both stand on sites that were previously occupied by buildings of special significance to Montreal. One of them, being built by developer David Azrieli, stands on the site of the demolished Van Horne house. Its twin across the street is being built by developer Joseph Kracauer on the site formerly occupied by the home of Isaac Walton Killam, the originator of the Canada Council.

Farther along Sherbrooke St., another tower of bronze reflecting glass is going up. It will serve as the new headquarters of the Alliance Mutual Life Insurance Company. The parallel-piped shape of the building is innovative in design, however, and the structure will be distinctive.

Of the new projects planned or already under way, several appear to offer definite benefit to the city. But too many others are unimaginative and unnecessary, high-rise blots on the city-scape.

Developments like Place Ville Marie and Place Bonaventure add excitement and vitality to the city center. But too many of the new projects add nothing but dollars to the developers' pockets and tend to turn the city into canyons of concrete filing cabinets.

The challenge of the next few years is to find methods of allowing the imaginative developers to work, while restraining the fast-buck artists as much as possible.

Chapter Five

What's the
Matter with Old McGill?

The demolition foreman wiped his brow in frustration.

"Look at that wall," he exclaimed. "Three walls down and the fourth still standing straight as a pine tree. They don't build them like that anymore."

It wasn't nostalgia that motivated the remark. It was simply that he had knocked down a lot of buildings and this one was giving him more trouble than most.

The building being razed was the Prince of Wales Terrace, a residential block of eight homes that stood on Sherbrooke St. at the corner of McTavish for 112 years until McGill University knocked it down in 1971. McGill's Samuel Bronfman Building stands on the site now, an unremarkable concrete box that lends but a fraction of the charm to Sherbrooke St. that the old terrace did.

The Prince of Wales Terrace had been built in 1859, probably by Sir George Simpson. Simpson was the governor-in-chief of all Hudson's Bay Company land—about a quarter of North America—and a large property owner in what was then the rural district around Sherbrooke St.

The terrace was named in honor of the prince who became Edward VII. He was in Montreal at the time for the opening of the new Victoria Bridge.

"The building was in the English architectural tradition of terraces," says author Edgar Andrew Collard, the greatest living expert on the history of Montreal. "You still find many tremendous terraces in London. The houses were all the same, and the block as a whole would make a monumental architectural impression. A person living in the Prince of Wales Terrace, while not living in an individual mansion, still had grandeur of dwelling. Guests arriving at the terrace were approaching an impressive building, massive, dignified, austere, yet pleasant."

An advertisement of the time guaranteed residents of the Prince of Wales Terrace "clear views and salubrious air forever." As befitted Montreal's most fashionable residence, the best people moved in. Members of the Molson family lived there, as did several other people who became closely connected with McGill University. They included Sir William Peterson, the McGill principal who raised the university to greatness, and Sir William Macdonald, the tobacco baron and benefactor extraordinaire.

Several such terraces were built in Montreal in the late 19th century; none are still standing. The Prince of Wales Terrace, perhaps the finest example of the style in the city, was the last to survive.

"I'd say the Prince of Wales Terrace was the most graceful example of Victorian architecture in Montreal," said Arthur Erickson, who graduated from McGill's School of Architecture and went on to design Simon Fraser University, theme pavilions at Expo 67 and the Canadian pavilion at the Osaka World's Fair.

Why was the building destroyed? Stanley Frost, McGill's vice-principal, administration and professional faculties, offers this rationale:

"We felt that the building had already been destroyed when the last unit was demolished to make way for a hotel. It would have

Prince of Wales Terrace, built c. 1860.
Demolished by McGill University in 1972

cost us, according to our study, $1.25 million to restore it as opposed to our new building which cost $4.7 million. It would have given us about one-third the floor space of the new building. If we'd restored it, what would we do with it? People don't want to use it. They're not interested in old buildings anymore."

A 1962 provincial government bill gave McGill University the right of expropriation in a large area of downtown Montreal. McGill now has control of the area bounded by Sherbrooke, University, McGregor and Peel and of the area bounded by McGregor, McTavish, Pine and Mountain. Within these districts are some of Montreal's finest surviving mansions, as well as the many fine buildings of the old campus itself.

Many of these older buildings have been put to alternate use by the university, for the time being at least. McGill, which is sensitive about the controversy created by the decision to demolish the Prince of Wales Terrace and other 19th century houses, likes to point this out.

"We're as sensitive as anyone else," says Vice-principal Frost. "We like old buildings to look at, and wherever possible we save them. For instance, we have made an arrangement with a developer who is restoring several houses on University St., with plans to build an apartment tower behind them."

The University St. restorations are excellent. The interiors of the houses have been transformed into modern apartments with a touch of elegance while the outsides have retained the solid Victorian greystone appearance. The exercise suggests that restoration of older low-rise buildings is viable, even in the downtown area.

McGill has also renovated and put to new use several of its own older buildings. The old Student Union on Sherbrooke St., designed early in this century by Montreal architect Percy Nobbs, was entirely refurbished to house a distinguished selection of artifacts from the McCord Museum collections. The old biology building on the campus was stripped of its labs and classrooms and outfitted to serve as administration offices. The Royal Victoria

College, designed by Bruce Price and built with funds supplied by Lord Strathcona, was transformed from outdated dormitories to classrooms and practice areas for the music faculty. A fine new concert hall with excellent acoustical quality was added to the building.

But the good work done by McGill has been largely offset by the buildings it has destroyed. University officials appear to have placed a low priority on preserving the character and green spaces of their campus and the immediate surrounding area.

The greatest loss was undoubtedly the Prince of Wales Terrace, but there have been others. In 1973, McGill knocked down three 19th century homes on University St., including Devonshire Cottage. Built of smooth, grey limestone blocks in 1861 by the Parkins family, Devonshire Cottage was a fine example of a North American adaptation of French Provincial style. It was flanked by two other greystone houses of equal charm.

Mansions on Peel and McGregor were demolished as well and in 1974 the university ignored a public outcry and knocked down three large homes on Redpath St. The houses were well beyond the university precinct but had been acquired in the 1960's, McGill said, because of an urgent and immediate need for space.

The mansions included Saxonhurst, built in the 1870's by Herbert Wallis, who was connected with the Grand Trunk Railway. A second house dated from the same period and the third from the turn of the century. All were handsome, imposing buildings; all retained intact their characteristic Victorian ornateness.

McGill used the houses briefly for classrooms. But in 1971, the university vacated them and left them vacant until they were knocked down three years later. University officials claimed there was no alternative as the buildings did not lend themselves to restoration and had been on the market for three years without attracting a buyer.

59

"The people who say don't pull these houses down don't have to pay the cost of keeping them," Professor Frost commented.

Despite McGill's protestations, however, the destruction of the Redpath St. buildings attracted heavy fire. John Howick, speaking for the nearby Redpath Place homeowners' group, objected to the loss of the mansions. He noted McGill's "duty to preserve the fine spots of the downtown" and lamented that the university "did not behave in a different way from the city's commercial enterprises." There was a flurry of letters to the editor in Montreal newspapers expressing similar sentiments and recalling a pledge made by McGill in August, 1973, that the houses would not be demolished.

Despite that promise, it took a demolition crew just one weekend in late February, 1974, to turn the greystone, brick and oak panelling into rubble. McGill has reportedly now leased the land to a developer who has plans for a 90-unit apartment complex.

McGill's destruction of old buildings is unhappily combined with a tendency towards replacing them with box-like structures of questionable architectural distinction.

"I regret that McGill's second period of growth has come at a time of very undistinguished architecture," says Prof. Frost. He blames much of the bland construction on the Quebec government, which provides grants for new buildings on the basis of a certain number of dollars per square foot.

"The provincial norms prevent us from doing what we might like," he explains. "The norms in Quebec are the lowest university construction norms in North America. We are required to produce the bare core of a building. We can't afford things like the teak panelling you'll find at the University of Toronto."

There is no sign of any change coming in the university's approach. At least some elements in the McGill administration regard the remaining mansions under the university's control, as well as some of the buildings on the campus itself, as a sort of land bank for future development.

A master plan published by the university in September, 1972, denotes the sites of several mansions as space available for future expansion. "Existing structures within the sites have been considered as disposable in the long term to allow for such development," says the eighth progress report of the Senate Committee on Development, in which the master plan was published.

Included in the list of buildings considered to be "disposable" in the long term are the 78-year-old McIntyre house on Peel St., which now houses a mental health unit; a red brick mansion on Drummond known as Davis house; two brick homes on Pine just east of the new, round McIntyre tower; and the 1893 Ross mansion, now Chancellor Day Hall, at the corner of McGregor and Peel.

This last mansion was designed by Bruce Price, the architect who built Windsor Station. It was owned by J.K.L. Ross whose horse, Sir Barton, was the first winner of the Triple Crown of racing in 1919.

The McGill master plan designates as disposable most of the east side of Peel St. between Sherbrooke and McGregor, which is one of the last unbroken Victorian street-sides in the city. Also targeted are the Presbyterian College on University at Milton (which is not now owned by the university) and the 74-year-old castle-like Marlborough Apartments at 570 Milton, owned by McGill as "investment property." Other properties, including the magnificent pink sandstone Pillow mansion (now called Hosmer house) on Drummond St. and Purvis Hall on Pine which was built by Imperial Tobacco boss Sir Mortimer Davis in 1905 and possibly designed by the celebrated Stanford White, have futures described as "undetermined" in the master plan. The greystone Duggan house on McTavish and Pine, built in 1860 by the yachtsman George Herrick Duggan, has been abandoned for some years now by the university and allowed to deteriorate. It cannot stand much longer.

The master plan also denotes several buildings on the old campus itself as developable sites. These include the Pulp and Paper building facing University St., an unpretentious three-storey stoneblock building dating from 1927; the old medical building at University and Pine; and, most alarming of all, the old Macdonald Chemistry Building.

The Chemistry Building is one of the familiar ornate greystone structures on the lower campus, built in 1896 through a gift from the tobacco baron. It is the companion building to the Macdonald Physics Building, where Lord Rutherford made his monumental contributions to nuclear science.

Morrice Hall, the old and unusual building just north of Redpath Hall, is the subject of a still unsettled debate. The Senate Committee makes a strong case for its demolition. But opposition has come from preservation groups both on and off campus.

The building is a visual delight. It has an excess of roof decorations, Gothic windows and a minaret on one corner. It contains an octagonally shaped room that is a miniature version of the Parliamentary Library in Ottawa. The building, which is certainly the most unorthodox structure on the McGill campus and one of the strangest in Montreal, was built around 1880 as an expansion move by the Presbyterian College.

McGill's most recent announcement on the fate of Morrice Hall said that it would be kept if "an engineering structural analysis be favourable and... a project group be able to recommend acceptable use of the space." By late 1974 the building remained empty, unpainted and uncared-for.

Another source for developable sites is the lawns and groves of the campus, and these have already been heavily encroached upon. Fully one-third of the open space of the lower campus has been built on in the past 10 years, and the green haven in the city center has now been severely compromised.

The Senate's master plan for future McGill development will not necessarily be followed. The official term for it is "an image to guide the planning process." McGill recently set up a special commission to study all university buildings and to recommend what to keep and what to replace. It is expected to report early in 1975.

But with further expansion of the university checked by tight government money and a shortage of students, McGill seems committed to a rationalization program that will consolidate facilities and put the emphasis on economy of operation.

There is an irony in this situation. Study in the field of restoration architecture is growing in significance in North America today. New York's Columbia University offers courses in the subject. But McGill, which has a living classroom for this field which is probably unrivalled on the continent, has ignored the subject and the potential use to which its old mansions could be put.

"It's our policy to get out of the old buildings," Vice-principal Frost says. "They are ruinously expensive to operate and not designed for academic purposes."

Taking the overview of the McGill situation, it seems that history, architecture and the social values provided by the beauty and unusualness of old buildings are minor considerations in determining the university's development policies. The old houses now in McGill's hands represent an important segment of Montreal's past, but the university's care of them and commitment to keeping them is, at best, minimal. Once elegant living quarters have been converted to classrooms with little care: blackboards nailed over oak-panelled walls, linoleum laid on hardwood floors, gardens neglected and conservatories abandoned.

McGill makes no commitments that any of these mansions or any of its campus buildings will remain part of the Montreal scene.

"The Faculty Club (the 1860 Baumgarten mansion on McTavish with its chain-suspended dance floor) and the key buildings on the campus are secure for our generation," says Prof. Frost. "I can't speak for 10 or 20 years from now."

Chapter Six

Buy a House, Board it Up

"Marvellous, unique, can't be duplicated."

The speaker was Jane Jacobs, celebrated urban expert. She had just completed a tour of the Milton-Park area in 1969, and was highly impressed with what she had seen.

"Montreal will destroy itself if it lets these areas of diverse activity go," she commented.

Three years later, four city blocks in the heart of Milton-Park resembled a lunar landscape. Bulldozers had moved in and flattened 255 homes and 20 small businesses. The Cité Concordia project was under way.

In many ways, the Concordia project is typical of urban renewal schemes in Montreal. Private enterprise dreams up a plan and civic authorities support it. The results are inevitable: rows of Victorian greystone homes are replaced by a complex of high-rise buildings and a community, a small corner of the fabric of Montreal society, disappears.

The Milton-Park area (more traditionally known as le Quartier Sainte-Famille) was an ideal spot for community growth. The row-houses that still characterize what is left of the area date from the turn of the century. They were solidly built, constructed of greystone quarried on the Island of Montreal.

Boarded-up house in Little Burgundy

The Slovenia Meat Market on St. Lawrence Boulevard

The area was originally middle class. But in recent years, its central location, low rentals and community warmth made it a favorite among workers, old people, immigrant groups and students. Unlike many of Montreal's communities, a considerable portion of its population was transient. But only the faces changed; the character of the residents, and thus of the community, remained constant.

But it is unlikely that many residents consciously thought of Milton-Park as the coherent neighborhood it was. People simply appreciated the well-preserved, human-scale buildings and the spacious but inexpensive homes they provided. They liked the old trees that lined the streets. They enjoyed the meeting places—the corner grocery stores, the restaurants, the tobacconists and the laundromats.

Milton-Park had a solid base—good housing in a good location. From that it evolved into a substantial community which met the needs of the people who lived there. It wasn't planned, but in many ways this worked to its advantage. It evolved free from the sterility that often characterizes planned communities and became instead a genuine "people place."

"This area is too good to be considered an urban renewal area," said a Montreal City Planning Department report when Milton-Park was intact. Then as now, the administration didn't listen to its own planners.

If a community is a natural thing, a place where people can live together without really being aware of it, then it is just as natural that neighbors should get together to react to a common threat. Such a threat became clear in Milton-Park in 1968. That's when it was revealed that a Montreal development firm, Concordia Estates Ltd., had quietly acquired 98 percent of the non-institutional property within the area bounded by Hutchison, Pine, Ste.-Famille and Milton. When it became clear the company planned to completely change the face of the area, the residents banded together and objected.

They objected to the fact that their homes and lifestyle would disappear. They objected when the city gave the lanes in the area to Concordia. They objected when the residents of 225 houses were evicted. They objected when those buildings stood empty for two and a half years before being bulldozed.

The objections gave many residents of Milton-Park a lesson in civic politics and earned some of them a night in jail. They cemented the community as only an exterior common threat could. But they didn't stop Concordia. Today, four years after the evictions, the project is under way.

The Milton-Park residents had numerous complaints about the way in which it all happened. They complained that Concordia had never consulted them as to whether they wanted the area renewed, never considered their objections, and, worst of all, planned a complex that was totally unrelated to the area and which was essentially meaningless to long-time residents of Milton-Park.

"Even if the project were a paradise it could not serve the needs of the people in the neighborhood," said city planner Anshel Melamed. "It is not for them."

The plans for Cité Concordia include a 23-storey office tower, a 500-room hotel and several "residential clusters" ranging in height from eight to 25 storeys. The rents in these buildings are expected to be two to three times those in the houses that disappeared. So even if some of the old Milton-Park residents did want to exchange a two-storey house with a fireplace for high-rise living, they probably couldn't afford it.

The development will also have secondary effects. Combined with the strange workings of the tax system, one development project can undo an entire area. Without specific protection, which does not seem to be forthcoming, all of old Milton-Park and the community it supports will disappear. It all amounts to another defeat for low-cost, low-density, friendly living in downtown Montreal. It also means the disappearance of more Victorian architecture and of another in-city community.

"How do I explain people gathering into communities?" sociology professor Kurt Jonassohn asks. "Let me turn that around. If people didn't form communities, then you'd have to do some explaining. Man is a social animal. He needs social interaction, he needs other people. What's the worst punishment somebody can get? Solitary confinement."

Jonassohn sees the emergence of communities within cities as a manifestation of man's social requirements. An individual has his family and friends but beyond that he is part of a circle of people—his neighbors and the people who service his area such as the paper-boy, the barber, the mailman. This makes him part of a familiar group of people within a defined territory.

This unity provides strength: strength to solve problems, strength to promote internal and external security. Exchanges of information through the community's meeting places—the churches, the taverns, the corner stores, the playgrounds—further this process.

Communities can be formed in a variety of ways. They may be created by physical boundaries—Point St. Charles was cut off from the rest of Montreal by the Lachine Canal and evolved in its own unique way. Or they may be formed through the common ethnic origin of the inhabitants, such as Chinatown or the old Jewish community around St. Urbain St.

Left alone, they grow and acquire integrity.

"Spontaneity is the key," says city planner Melamed. "You don't find life in planned communities or planned cities. Look at Place Ville Marie and St. Catherine St. St. Catherine is neon, honky-tonk, exuberant. PVM is cold. Look at Brasilia, the prototype of the planned city. Everything was provided for, yet it is deadly dull. No surprises.

"The excitement of Montreal is largely unplanned."

Community development is very much a function of physical setting. By its very design, housing of the type found in Milton-Park and many of the other older areas of Montreal promotes community growth.

It has to do with having a "direct means of interchange with the common area," architect and University of Montreal professor Melvin Charney explains.

"The older houses have a door that opens directly on the street, the common area, and windows and balconies that look directly out onto it. This is something that is missing from contemporary high-rises."

Studies have indicated that people living in high-rise buildings have fewer acquaintances in their immediate neighborhood than those living in low-rise and medium-rise buildings.

"Nobody likes to live in a large, anonymous environment where nobody knows anybody or talks to anybody," sociologist Jonassohn says. "But since the Second World War there has been this notion of bigness, of efficiency. Thus you have the giant department store and the supermarket. But they were successful partly because they were novelties. I think now we are seeing the return of the little store. A few years ago, all the little stores were complaining that they were being killed by the big ones. Now look at all the little stores, like the little fruit stores on St. Catherine St., that have resurfaced. That's a complete reversal of the trend and an indication that the population is rejecting mass values.

"Why? Because the little places are personal, not anonymous. You can walk in and say: 'What have you got that's good today?' You can't do that in a supermarket. And we must not forget that people meet each other in stores, that they are often as much community centers as stores.

"The same idea holds true in housing. The trend I see in the student population is that they like old houses, not new ones. The new ones are too box-like, not built for comfortable living. They like houses that are, by modern standards, badly laid out, full of nooks and crannies.

"I think we can also see something here in the popularity of Old Montreal," Jonassohn continues. "What makes it attractive is that it has history, something that predates us. As I walk along Dorchester, I can remember when practically everything was built. But in Old Montreal, you have a feeling of tradition. Also, things are of human scale. You can't get close to Place Ville Marie, but you can to Old Montreal. It's a much more conducive setting for human interaction.

"That's why I think bigness was a brief phase. It doesn't really work. The big housing developments either turn into slums or, in the case of a luxury apartment like the Port-Royal, it becomes a place to sleep for people whose social forms take place somewhere else."

Jonassohn sees changes coming: "People in the city used to be moved around and they used to say: 'Well, that's life.' Now they protest."

Indeed, protest against bigness and intrusion by governments and large development firms is starting to become a way of life in Montreal. In recent years the city has seen a proliferation of community-based groups in places like Milton-Park, Lower Westmount, Point St. Charles and Little Burgundy. Groups have been created to stop a highway in Lachine, to save Windsor Station, to preserve a green space in Pointe Claire and for a variety of other purposes.

These groups have a common aim: community government from the bottom up instead of from the top down. Given the right circumstances, they can grow in importance to the point where, as in Toronto, they can actually wrest control of the municipal administration from establishment politicians and impose severe new restraints on developers.

This is still a long way from happening in Montreal, however. By late 1974, the administration still placed a low priority on the preservation of neighborhoods, and communities are still having a hard time winning recognition. Poorer areas, where speculators are attracted by low property values and where, paradoxically, communities are often more vital, tend to suffer more than affluent districts.

"I remember when I first got into this business around 1960," says one Montreal architect. "If we had a project, we looked for the land that was the cheapest. We simply never thought about the people."

The City of Montreal Planning Department would like to see characteristic neighborhoods preserved, and its emphasis is now on keeping communities together. But what the Planning Department thinks and the Drapeau administration does are often two different things. In fact, Montreal's zoning laws and property tax structure almost seem to have been designed with block-busting and the destruction of neighborhoods in mind.

"Let's say Concordia builds," said Ed Zackon, chairman of the urban renewal sub-committee of the now defunct Montreal Council of Social Agencies. "This will make the land values in the adjacent areas rise quite a lot. Therefore, in 5 to 20 years it will be extremely valuable land. These increased values in the adjacent areas will make it 'necessary' to build more and more high-rises, and this will spread beyond the immediate area."

This phenomenon is now clearly visible in several areas of Montreal. In the Lincoln Ave. area, where high-rises are proliferating, the existing housing stock is mainly owned by speculators or developers. They allow their properties to fall into disrepair, anticipating eventual demolition. The same situation can be seen in the east end around the new Radio-Canada building, where "for sale" signs and boarded-up houses are appearing as never before.

"There's a speculator's ploy called abandonment," explains architect Charney. "You buy a house and board it up. It's an announcement that the neighborhood is finished. Montreal is the only city in Canada where they can get away with it."

The Quebec government has acknowledged the existence of neighborhoods in its newly-reorganized social welfare program, which is community-based. But there is no legal constraint of any sort in provincial law against the destruction of established communities by outsiders. And the province itself has been one of the leading offenders, ramming its east-west autoroute through the center of Montreal. The road cut communities like Lower Westmount in half and eventually took a toll of close to 3,000 homes.

The federal government, for its part, pretends that neighborhoods don't even exist.

"Residents are no doubt interested in maintaining their environment," Public Works Minister C.M. Drury said in March, 1974. "But they want it at no cost to themselves. Why should the federal taxpayer support the enjoyment of a small group of people?"

Ottawa's actions are as cold as Drury's words. The construction of Maison de Radio-Canada required the destruction of 1,250 homes—the complete annihilation of a viable east-end community. And the new federal complex now on the drawing board, Place Guy Favreau, will rise from the rubble of over half of what's left of Montreal's Chinatown.

The recent history of Montreal communities is a sad one. Many of the most colorful and characteristic of them have literally disappeared, bulldozed away by "progress."

Some of them—Griffintown is a good example—were simply zoned off the face of the earth.

Griffintown was an old Irish residential area, just south of the city center. Like several other communities, it was built around the factories that lined the Lachine Canal. Because there were factories already there, the city zoned the area industrial and set out to discourage housing.

"But that didn't work, because all the companies were moving out to the suburbs," one Griffintown native recalls. "So they chased out the people but didn't get the factories either."

Today what was Griffintown is mostly parking lots. A few people still live there, but an in-city suburb of 3,000 to 4,000 people has been reduced to a few hundred.

"Maybe the place was kind of falling apart," the Griffintowner says. "But it wasn't a bad place to live. I'll tell you, when you were born there and you go back and see all the parking lots, it hurts."

Little Burgundy, to the west of Griffintown, isn't what it used to be either. It lost some fine old churches to the autoroute and much of its housing to less-than-successful urban renewal schemes. Solid two-storey and three-storey brick row-housing in the district is still being discarded at an alarming rate.

Victoriatown is an example of a community that has completely disappeared. It once stood at the foot of the Victoria Bridge, but was rubbed out in the mid-1960's to make way for the Autostade and several Expo 67 buildings.

Further west, St. Henri remains an interesting and workable mix of commercial and residential properties. But there are a disturbing number of "for sale" signs going up and boarded-up houses are on the increase. There may be trouble ahead, but much of the area still looks good. Jacques Cartier Square, off St. Antoine St., is surrounded by lovely homes and may be the most attractive town square remaining in Montreal.

Point St. Charles, bordered on the north by the Lachine Canal, is the most celebrated "poor" area in the city. It has been the subject of numerous reports and studies over the years, ever since the CNR and other large companies cut back staff and saddled the area with higher than viable levels of unemployment. But, it never received the help it really needed—schools and a good housing program.

"I think there's somebody up in City Hall who's decided to keep this area poor," said one long-time Point resident. "The old housing is so bad you only live there if you can't afford to move out. And the new city housing, well, your rent is decided on what your income is. That means if you make too much, you're not allowed to live here. You've got to be poor."

But what the Point lacks in physical amenities it makes up for in community spirit. It is one of the most closely-knit communities in the city, although the long-time Irish residents and the newer French-Canadian segment remain separate.

"A lot of people have moved out in the last 15 years, but I'll tell you something," the Point resident said. "A guy I know bought a $35,000 house in Beloeil. But once a week he's got to come back here and hang around the pool hall. He's got a nice house out there, but you couldn't replace the old neighborhood."

Chinatown's story is somewhat different. There were Chinese people living in the area in the 1860's, and after the disbanding of the Chinese work crews when the CPR was completed in 1885, Montreal's Chinatown expanded greatly. Eventually, the community included sections of Clark, St. Urbain, Chenneville, Lagauchetière, Dorchester and Vitre streets, with the center being the familiar restaurant and grocery store area at Clark and Lagauchetière.

But in the 1960's, renewal schemes began to reduce Chinatown. The widening of Dorchester Blvd. took many homes, as did the east-west autoroute. Many families had to move away from old Chinatown, some to the "Chinatown suburbs" north of Sherbrooke Street.

Today, the federal government is poised for what will probably be the coup de grace for Chinatown. Place Guy Favreau will cover the area bounded by Dorchester, Lagauchetière, St. Urbain and Jeanne Mance, immediately to the south of the giant Complexe Desjardins which is now nearing completion. The construction of Place Guy Favreau will mean the demolition of all three Chinatown churches: the Chinese Presbyterian Church, the Chinese Pentecostal Church and the Chinese Catholic Mission. Part of the latter is located in an ancient stone building, which historical experts believe may have originally been the mid-19th century Cote St. Presbyterian Church. The churches aren't the only victims. Place Guy Favreau has already displaced Chinatown's main employer, the Wong Wing Noodle Company.

"I'd like to see Chinatown stay here," says Wong Wing president Marcel Wong. "So would the City Planning Department. But it involves so much money. I'd like to see the city designate the boundaries of Chinatown and control it so it wouldn't get into the hands of speculators, so it would remain in the hands of the local citizenry.

"But how much hope is there? We're down to one block now (Lagauchetière to Vitre) and how much hope is there for one block?"

Wong wanted his factory to remain in Chinatown. He got promises of land to replace the property that was expropriated, but promises were all he got. Finally, he moved his factory out of the area.

"I would like to have stayed because there's a great deal more to Chinatown than you see," he said. "There's the churches and the social organizations and the family associations (Lee, Hum and Wong) which operate sort of as banks. A lot of Chinese people have had to move out of this area, but you come here on a Sunday morning. You'll see how important this area is."

"The church has to stay here," says Father Thomas Tou of the Chinese Catholic Mission who, like other church leaders, received promises of alternate land sites from the government but no more. "The city has knocked down here, knocked down there, and they never build anything. This is bad for me because I have lost so many parishioners. But I have to stay here because this is the only common place for all the Chinese in Montreal."

Father Tou is staying in the area. He's building a new church at St. Lawrence and Vitre, but at a cost. Government expropriation gave him $9.50 a square foot for his old church and community center. The new land cost $17.50 a foot.

Despite the injustices done to the Chinese community, the federal government is going ahead with its scheme. René Menkes, the Montreal architect who has already contributed 2020 University and the rising Centre Capitol to the city, says his firm is designing the complex. The government is demolishing buildings in the area as soon as they get hold of them. Already some of the solid stone commercial buildings on Lagauchetière have been knocked down, as well as the old home of the Wong Wing Noodle Company.

Lower Westmount is the community story that has come closest to a happy ending—several times.

In the 1960's, the province expropriated and knocked down 250 homes in Lower Westmount for the east-west autoroute. Selby St., for instance, disappeared almost entirely. The City of Westmount seized the opportunity to propose a "comprehensive development" for the area west of Atwater between Dorchester and St. Antoine.

The plan included a four-storey blank wall facing St. Antoine St. Residents fought the plan and won. It was called off.

"Everything was fine until one morning we woke up and found expropriation notices from Hydro-Quebec in the mail," Lower Westmount Citizens Committee president Fred Leclaire remembers. "They wanted to tear down St. Antoine St. (a street lined with solid greystone houses) for a new plant. We fought that too and eventually they built on a park down the street and tore down only 12 residences.

"Then we were all right again until late 1970 when the Highways Department unveiled a plan for a huge access ramp down Greene Ave. Well, we'd won against the urban renewal plan and we weren't going to lose to the highway. The City of Westmount got involved on this one and it was stopped."

In early 1974, the outlook for Lower Westmount was rosy. The city hired architect Michael Fish to do a survey of the area and Joe Baker's Community Design Workshop was approached about rehabilitating some of the houses on Greene Ave.

But by mid-1974, the picture had dimmed again. The province is tight-lipped on the subject, but there are reports that the houses on Greene Ave. will not be repaired and that yet more houses are in danger of being demolished for construction of a service road alongside the expressway.

A community that is not doing well is the area around Lincoln Ave. A long-established district of greystone row houses and three to six-storey apartments centered around the shops of St. Catherine St. between Guy and Atwater, the area fell victim to the city's zoning laws in the early 1960's. Because there were residences in the area, it was zoned residential. Because high-rises bring more tax dollars than low-rises, it was zoned for high-rises. The result was an invitation to speculators, which they took advantage of.

Today the area is peppered with high-rises, some almost elegant but others distressingly cheap. Few streets—Baile and Seymour are notable exceptions—retain much of their old-style charm.

Speculators own much of what is left of the old housing. Predictably, decay is much in evidence. In a decade, the area has evolved from a comfortable, human-scale neighborhood to something approaching a high-rise jungle.

The city administration has watched this proliferation of 20th century structures on a 19th century street plan with apparent indifference. The district is now an urbanist's nightmare. The only park that remains in the entire area is Cabot Park—a little bit of green space perpetually ringed by idling MTC buses.

Another district in danger is St. Louis Square, one of Montreal's most attractive downtown residential areas. The buildings are two or three-storey homes, most of them dating from the Victorian era. They are constructed of red brick or greystone and many display adventurous architecture.

Domes with tiny flagpoles, wrought-iron decorations and pinnacles dominate the skyline of St. Louis Square. Everywhere the lightness and spatial considerations that characterize Montreal's older residential areas are in evidence.

The area has long been a favorite spot for Montreal's French-speaking intelligentsia and artistic set. More recently, it has become home to dozens of immigrant Portuguese, who in many instances have upgraded some of the less-well-cared-for surrounding streets.

In March, 1974, it was discovered that a Swiss firm, Procan Finanz, had well-advanced plans to build two 23-storey towers on Sherbrooke St. between Laval and St. Denis—the block immediately to the south of St. Louis Square. The site is the former property of Les Soeurs de Bon-Pasteur. A college stood there for a century or more, saw brief service as an Expo 67 hotel, and then burned down.

A citizens' group was promptly formed to fight the towers, which would have been completely out of character with the area. Moreover, based on past experience, construction of two giant high-rises in the area would have brought powerful pressures to bear on residents of the square to sell out to developers.

"We're not against development," said Michelle Jodoin-Keaton of the Comité des Citoyens Faubourg Cherrier. "But we think development should respect the local area and not upset the residents."

To prove its point, the Comité prepared an alternate scheme and took it and their protest to a Montreal Executive Committee meeting. To everyone's surprise, the City called a halt to the project. That's where the situation stood in mid-1974. There are no guarantees for the future, but there's still sunlight in St. Louis Square.

Down on the Main, they're hoping for similar protection from the city.

In recent years, the Main—officially St. Lawrence Blvd.—has lost its notoriety and regained its image as a street of many fine, small shops. But some of the Main's merchants feel threatened by large-scale development to the west (Concordia) and the east (Sherbrooke and St. Denis streets), as well as by the less-than-adventurous attitude of some of the older store-owners. The Main may soon become the new target for developers—but for the moment, all the color and ethnic diversity remain, making the street one of Montreal's major assets.

"The people who are still interested in personal shopping come to the Main," says Peter Vizel, who is in the imported woollens business and who is founder of the Save the Main movement. "You know, there isn't a chain store or a department store on the street. If you want fish or different kinds of olives or fresh fruit—really fresh fruit—or sauerkraut out of a barrel, the Main is the only place.

"Kids go to Morocco and come back and talk about how they bartered for things in the markets there. You can still do that here!"

The Main is the shopping center for various ethnic communities around St. Lawrence Blvd., but the apparent prosperity of many of the stores suggests that Montrealers from other areas are catching on as well.

Nearby ethnic communities include the old Jewish area around St. Urbain St., celebrated by Mordecai Richler. The nationalities are changing these days, however—you now find the Macelleria Italiana and the Knosos Meat Market down the street from Wilensky's Light Lunch. But the area remains vital and will continue to be so unless the developers move in.

The Main is a community—the kind of community that people must have in the core area of a city if they are to relate to things about them. Communities like the Main, and Chinatown, and Milton-Park have a right to survive.

Short of large-scale government intervention, there is only one way that can happen. The communities themselves must have control over any and all developments proposed for their areas.

Chapter Seven

The Saving of Crescent St.

The area around Stanley, Mountain, Crescent and Bishop streets is a unique urban playground of bars, bistros, restaurants and boutiques.

It is one of Montreal's most colorful and exciting quarters, full of exuberance and spontaneity. It is a place for people, both day and night—somewhere to talk, play chess, pick up a date or get quietly drunk.

The Crescent St. district offers excitement and flavor at any hour. Yet until June 11, 1974, there was a real danger that the whole area would be developed out of existence in the name of progress.

Several big developers were well advanced with plans to completely change the character of the district. Only a sudden, and totally unexpected move by city council prevented it all from happening.

Without a word of advance warning, the Drapeau administration announced its intention to bring in a by-law to protect not only the bistro-boutique quarter but a sizeable area around it as well.

To the surprise of both developers and preservationists, council acted on the recommendation of the executive committee to introduce a by-law calling for a 60-day freeze on the issuing of new construction permits in the area.

This was followed up with regulations banning new parking lots in the area and introducing spot zoning as a means to preserve existing low-rise buildings. Under the system, no building of more than 12 storeys will be permitted in the district, and lower limits have been applied to especially vulnerable sections.

Council's action was the first civic response to the need for area preservation since Old Montreal had been declared an historic quarter more than a decade earlier. By proposing the new by-law, a city administration that had previously bent over backwards to encourage new development, formally recognized that financial considerations had to take second place at some point to the social and environmental needs of the city.

The Crescent St. area is unmatched in Canada and its loss would have been a tragedy for Montreal. Other cities have similar districts—Toronto's Yorkville and Vancouver's Gastown—but they lack the vibrant atmosphere of the Montreal quarter.

Gastown is an admirable example of what can be done with a slum area but it lacks ambience and most of its structures are new buildings trying to look old.

Yorkville is dominated by commercially chic shops, but is dead after midnight.

Crescent St. and its neighbors are just coming alive at that hour. And they stay alive 24 hours a day because the area is still partly residential. People live in apartments above the bars and boutiques, and there are doctors and dentists mixed in with the antique shops. The character of the area changes several times a day—quiet in the morning, crowded with businessmen and secretaries at lunch, bustling with fashion-conscious shoppers in mid-afternoon, swinging after five with the cocktail-hour crowd, busy with diners in the evening and jumping with the in-crowd into the wee small hours.

Victorian greystones on Crescent Street

It's a district that is loved by Montrealers and tourists alike. They come to window-shop for exclusive Parisian couture and to buy roses from a long-haired flower girl. They come to browse in the elegant antique shops and to hear the street musicians. They congregate at the Rainbow Bar and Grill on Stanley St. for a chess game, or watch old movies at the Annex on Bishop St. They wander in and out of discothèques and bars. They sit in sidewalk cafés drinking Spanish coffee and watching the passers-by.

The streets cater to all tastes. There's hamburgers, dished out by Carol and Nick Iadeluca who have been doing it every day for 18 years. There are sumptuous restaurants such as the temple of haute cuisine dedicated to the sensuous, gallant king of France, Henri IV. Diners show up in evening dress to try the *spécialités de la maison* at Les Halles, while just across the street other restaurants cater to blue-jeaned bikers.

You can buy just about anything in the quarter—genuine pine Canadiana, erotic sexual aids, antique silver, needlework patterns, original oil paintings, fine men's clothes, flowered hats. When the shopping is over, you can adjourn to the Sir Winston Churchill Pub, once declared the best bar in the world by the International Airline Pilots Association.

The Pub, as it is affectionately known to regulars, was the first bar on Crescent St. It was opened in 1967 by John Vago, who also owns the Casa Pedro and the Boiler Room.

Before the appearance of The Pub, Crescent St. had been a quiet residential area. Its quaint, greystone row-houses were home to middle-class Montrealers, as they had been since the turn of the century when most of the structures in the area were built.

But once The Pub opened, things were never the same again. Other businessmen saw a good thing and started to move in. Sleepy Crescent St. became swinging Crescent St. The same process was taking place on other streets in the district—Stanley, Mountain, Bishop.

The inevitable development pressures followed. As real-estate speculators saw how desirable the area was becoming they started to buy up property for re-sale to high-rise developers. Property evaluations began to rise, and owners of three and four-storey buildings suddenly began to find their tax bills increasing astronomically. High-rises began to appear on Mountain and Stanley. Some large-scale development began on Bishop St., and low-rise buildings were demolished for parking lots.

Only two blocks of Crescent, from St. Catherine to Sherbrooke, remained low-rise by the time the city moved to halt further high-rise development. And only one block, that between de Maisonneuve and Sherbrooke, still retains most of its original buildings.

That one block of Crescent St. is the most perfectly preserved example of a particular style of turn-of-the-century architecture in the downtown core. But until city council acted, the block was seriously threatened with demolition and redevelopment.

Trizec Corporation, Canada's largest development firm, had started assembling land in the area. The company had acquired the Sherbrooke Apartments at the corner of Crescent and Sherbrooke, Montreal's first apartment building. It also bought two Crescent St. buildings behind the apartment house and took options on sites all the way to de Maisonneuve including a lane and a parking lot which opens on to Bishop St.

One of the corporation's employees, who has administered the properties for years, says plans have been in the works for a hotel complex on the site. Trizec denies it has any such plans, although it makes it clear that redevelopment in the area was planned eventually. One executive of the company described the Sherbrooke Apartments as "really run down—just cheap office space for a bunch of doctors and dentists." He added: "We'll eventually replace it with something more in character with the area." The fact that the apartments are of the same age, height and architectural style as the rest of Crescent St. "doesn't mean they are in the same character," he continued. Anyway, he can't figure out what people find so attractive about the street in the first place: "I think it's a mess."

Ben Cummings, who administers Trizec's property in the area, agrees. He doesn't think there is anything on the street worth saving because "they've put shop fronts on everything."

While Trizec denies any plans for Crescent St., the company cannot deny that it has been assembling land there. Since the firm is known for large commercial developments, and not for preservation, the suspicions of many Montrealers about its intentions in the quarter are understandable.

But the city council's limitations on new construction have stymied whatever plans Trizec may have had. It doesn't make much economic sense to tear a three-storey building down in order to put up a four-storey one in its place which is all the new by-law will allow.

Another developer affected by the new by-law is Isaac Gelber, a man who is less secretive than Trizec about his plans. Gelber owns almost all of the bottom third of Crescent St., between Dorchester and St. Catherine. The few sites he doesn't control include the YWCA building and a parking lot at the corner of St. Catherine St. The lot is South American owned, although Gelber says he is negotiating to buy it.

Once the property was his, Gelber's idea was to demolish all the low-rise buildings on both sides of the street and to put up a gigantic complex. This would have consisted of three 28-storey apartment towers containing 1,000 bachelor flats on the east side, and a matching garage with space for 1,200 cars on the west side. Access to the garage would have been from Bishop St., where Gelber also owns property.

Gelber acquired his Crescent St. holdings about six years ago in an estate sale. He recently painted several of the buildings garish red, yellow and blue, hiding their state of dilapidation.

"Paint's cheap, brings people to the area, so we're going to do more of it," he says.

Gelber's plans for the area would have been blocked by existing zoning laws, even if city council hadn't moved. That part of Crescent St. is not zoned for high-rise buildings, although Gelber said he planned on "changing" that to build his towers.

"I have to put high-rises to pay the taxes," he says, estimating his property is worth $40.00 a square foot.

Gelber is a typical Montreal developer. He is involved in so many companies that it is almost impossible to keep track of them. The building directory at 1247 Guy St. lists at least 22 firms that are run from Gelber's office. They include Gelber Enterprises, Gelber and Gelber, Gelfran, Gelber Industries, Gelber Investments, Gelber Realty Corp., Harvard Investments, Canada Leasing, Dorchester Leasing, Dorchester Realty Regd., Crescent Leasing, Mackay Leasing, Masson Holdings, Restaurant Investments, Stanley Leasing, Tullmas Associates, Loan Rite Corp., Joe's Steak House, McGregor Leasing, Industrial Export Co., Canada Compound Co., and Bishop Leasing.

Tenants in Gelber's buildings on Crescent St. say there have been attemps to persuade them to leave and to move to other areas of the city. Some claim the landlord refused to renew leases or to make minor repairs.

Similar tactics have been experienced by a number of tenants on Bishop St.

In the spring of 1974, developer Abe Fleming was taken to court by Rod and Maureen Davies, a young couple living in one of five century-old greystones owned by Fleming. It was being demolished to make way for another parking lot.

The couple lived on the two top floors of the building, and decided to do what they could to save it. They took out an injunction against Fleming, claiming they had not been given proper notice of termination of their lease under the new Quebec rental code.

Under the code, landlords must give 90 days notice if a lease is to be terminated. Tenants must also give 90 days notice if they do not intend to renew. If neither party gives notice, the lease is automatically renewed for another term.

The Davies' claimed that because they did nothing, the lease should have been extended. But they lost their case after Fleming showed in court that the five buildings were classed as rooming houses and the leases were commercial rather than residential, thus requiring only 30 days notice of termination.

The couple lost the case and were forced to move out. The building was demolished and Fleming won the battle. He has since been operating a parking lot on the site, even though the new city by-law supposedly prohibits the creation of any more parking lots in the area.

After the Davies court case, they and other residents of Bishop St. decided they'd had enough and formed a tenants' association to do battle with two developers planning projects at the corner of de Maisonneuve.

On the east side of Bishop, Yale Properties, acting under the name of Curzon, bought Bishop Court in March, 1974. This is a stately red and beige brick building containing 18 apartments. Residents of the building at first were asked to vacate their flats so "renovations" could be made on the 70-year-old structure. None of them received written eviction notices, as required by law. Representatives of the firm, which is run by the seven Mashaal brothers, frequently visited tenants in the building in an effort to persuade them to move.

When one tenant filed a legal protest with the Quebec Rental Board, company vice-president Fred Mashaal filed a counter suit. He said the existing lease should not be extended because the building was going to be demolished. He then went to court, demanded and received a demolition permit for the building. Once he had it, he announced the building wasn't going to be demolished after all. Obtaining the demolition permit was the "only way" to evict the tenants, he contended.

But the Quebec rental code, which came into effect in January, 1974, states that tenants cannot be evicted for purposes of demolition or renovation until the end of their leases. Even then, they must be informed in writing of the landlord's intention 90 days in advance.

Since coming into force, this law has been used by thousands of Quebec tenants to hold off attempts by landlords to force them out. But the message doesn't seem to have gotten through to some developers yet.

Across from Bishop Court, tenants of the Royal George Apartments were also asked to move by the new owners of their building, Gipala Properties. The company purchased the Royal George in March, 1974, gaining possession of the only terra cotta building in Montreal, an ornately facaded structure built in 1912 that was the first high-rise to have an electric elevator.

Tenants in the building were told by the new landlords that their apartments were to be converted into offices and asked if they wouldn't like to move.

None of the tenants in the Royal George or Bishop Court are sure what is going to happen to them or to their buildings. But the city's new by-law has given them hope that their apartment blocks will survive and that the inroads of the developers will stop.

Helen Gougeon's reaction is typical of residents in the area. She owns La Belle Cuisine gourmet shop on lower Bishop, facing Abe Fleming's newly-created empty lot.

"We are all concerned about the diminishing charm of our street," she says. "It is one of the last blocks left and people have invested a lot in restaurants and shops here."

Businesses on Crescent St. also represent a large investment. John Vago, one of the street's first entrepreneurs, says the personal element has made the area successful and popular.

"People come from all over the world to admire what we have done here," he says. "People who have businesses here are proud of what they do and most of them are making a profit.

"It's a center of life, a human street. And it's going to last forever."

Chapter Eight

Greystones
and Movie Palaces

"Windsor Station—Finest in Creation!"

So read the banner William Van Horne draped across his new station when it first opened 85 years ago. It was no groundless boast.

Windsor Station was the terminus of the CPR, the company that had just built a railroad clear across a continent, a technological feat comparable today to putting a man on the moon.

In building the railway, Canadian Pacific provided the tie that made a string of settlements into a nation. "It was the CPR," wrote an observer at the time, "that breathed life into the nostrils of Canada."

The station itself turned out to be a watershed in Canadian building design. It provided the model for what came to be known as the Canadian Railroad Chateau Style, possibly the most distinctive school ever developed by Canadian architects.

Scores of little railroad stations across the country took their inspiration from it, as did many major buildings. The architects of the station, Bruce Price, Edward and William Maxwell, John Watts, L. Fennings Taylor and W.S. Painter, carried the style on to the Viger Station and Hotel (now City of Montreal offices) and

Royal Victoria Hospital and College. Other major buildings constructed in the style include the Chateau Frontenac in Quebec City, and hotels at Banff Springs, Lake Louise, Calgary and Winnipeg.

The importance of Windsor Station's ties to history should be enough to guarantee it a permanent place in Montreal's city scape. But its ties to the people of Montreal are just as significant. Thousands of immigrants stepped from the platforms of the station into new lives in Canada. Young Canadians left the station for the battlefields of two world wars. To commuters, the station has been and remains the starting point for everyday life in Montreal.

Yet the fate of Windsor Station was in doubt for some time. In 1971, Canadian Pacific Ltd. was ready to go ahead with a major redevelopment program for the 15-acre site bounded by Dorchester, Peel, St. Antoine and Mountain, excluding St. George's Anglican Church. Despite the station's intimate ties to Canadian history, CP was prepared to demolish it as part of the scheme.

The threat to the station led to the formation of a preservationist group known as Friends of Windsor Station. The uproar raised by the organization, and the strong public response to it, were important elements in CP Ltd.'s decision to rethink the whole project. By late 1974, there was evidence that the company had at last accepted the idea of retaining at least the Peel St. façade of the station. But no public commitment had yet been made and no level of government had demanded that such action be taken.

"No matter what CP does," says a prominent Montreal architect, "they'll never get as well-made a building as Windsor Station. And for my money, they'll never get a handsomer one."

Windsor Station has another intimate tie to the city, one seldom noticed by Montrealers. That is the grey limestone of which it is constructed.

Much of the Montreal area is underlain with this rock, which geologists call Trenton limestone. For centuries it provided the building material for the city. As New York has its brownstone, Montreal has its greystone.

*Canadian Pacific's Windsor Station,
built between 1884 and 1913*

95

As can be seen in Old Montreal or in the ancient towers on Sherbrooke St., the stone was first used in whatever shapes nature had provided. But as New World masonry developed, so did the sophistication with which the greystone was used. It was cut into rough-edged blocks for Windsor Station. It was elegantly carved for Notre-Dame Church. It was sliced into enormous squares to line the Lachine Canal and used in a thousand other ways to provide building blocks for Montreal's mansions and distinctive greystone row-housing.

But today, steel and concrete have replaced stone as a building material. Montreal will never have any more greystone buildings than it has now—an obvious and valid reason for saving the best of what's left.

Thousands of greystone buildings have been torn down in the past few years. There were famous mansions like the Van Horne house and the Killam house and large buildings like the Balmoral Hotel on Notre Dame St., which was demolished in 1974 by Marathon Realties, a subsidiary of CP Ltd. There were churches and convents. There were the blocks of greystone houses in Milton-Park and in the east end where the CBC building now stands.

The decline of greystone as a building material and the proliferation of reinforced concrete construction in Montreal is a major reason why the city is losing its distinctive appearance and rapidly assuming the look of all other North American urban centers.

There's an irony here. Mayor Drapeau's ambition to make Montreal a tourist capital is based largely on the city's old-world charm. But the tourist boom has led to an emphasis on mid-town hotel construction, and this construction has come at the expense of many of the greystone buildings that gave Montreal the old-world look the mayor prizes so highly.

There are many reasons to preserve a building. They include the significance of the building material, historical connections, architectural importance, harmony with surroundings, beauty and the insights it might provide of life in another age. Often, it can be important to preserve not just a single structure, but an entire area.

"There's always the danger of a single building being surrounded by towers," says Judge Kenneth Mackay of the Viger Commission. "Look at Old Montreal. A whole area was preserved, and you can really get a feeling of what Montreal was like in the 1830's and 1840's."

Unfortunately, the downtown streets of Montreal today offer a jumbled appearance. There may be a row of high-rises with odd three-storey greystone mixed in, or a row of older houses with a high-rise stuck in the middle. The city streets are testimony to a lack of planning and historical perspective. Only a few downtown areas retain a coherent appearance. Crescent St. between Sherbrooke and de Maisonneuve is one; the east side of Peel up from Sherbrooke is another.

"It would be nice if the city could keep some areas of low-rise housing in the central part of the city," one troubled citizen said. "After all, there are people who want to live downtown and don't' want to live in a high-rise."

With larger buildings, ones that have outlived their original use, the key to preservation is recycling. The city administration, for instance, uses the old Viger Station and Hotel and the 130-year-old Bonsecours Market for offices. Corby's uses its Sherbrooke St. mansion for office space and receptions. The old Maisonneuve Market now serves as a police station.

But many fine buildings have been knocked down before they have had a chance for a new life. This is partly because the city's zoning and tax laws are geared in favor of demolition and new construction instead of renovation. The Capitol Theatre, for instance, had found new life as a medium-sized rock concert hall, but the fact that it was taxed as prime downtown land contributed to its early demise.

Conservation groups have been increasingly drawing attention to the need for changed laws and an attitude favoring renovation over demolition and new construction. There are, after all, still areas and buildings in Montreal worth preserving. In some cases, they may be familiar landmarks like Windsor Station. In others, they may be structures or streetscapes people walk by every day without noticing—until one day they've gone.

Some examples:—

St. James St.: "The Street" has been described as a "glossary of Canadian architecture." The blocks from St. Lawrence Blvd. to McGill St. used to form the banking headquarters of Canada. Although many of the major banks have now moved uptown to the Place Ville Marie area, St. James St. remains a living showplace of commercial building from the mid-19th century to the present.

The oldest structure on the street is the Bank of Montreal building, the small columned and domed building on Place d'Armes. It dates from 1846. Later additions include a rear wing by Stanford White, done around the turn of the century, and a new wing built in 1960 which replaced Montreal's old and ornate head post office.

Immediately across from the Bank of Montreal is The Street's newest address: the tall, shiny head office of the Banque Canadienne Nationale.

Victorian ornateness reached its peak on St. James St., and may still be seen in such gems as the Nesbitt Thomson Building (1875) and Molson's Bank (1875), now a branch of the Bank of Montreal.

Other old-timers on The Street include the Guaranty Trust Building (1865), the Jones Heward Building (1850), the City and District Bank (1873), and the Ottawa Building (1861). In all, more than 20 buildings on St. James St. date from the 19th century.

Perhaps the most magnificent structure of all is the Royal Bank of Canada Building, erected in 1927. No expense was spared in its construction, as the fine attention to detail and the generous use of gold leaf attest. The building was taken over by Trizec Corporation when the Royal Bank moved its head office uptown to Place Ville Marie.

Other contestants for the title of most magnificent structure include the columned Canadian Imperial Bank of Commerce Building (1907) and, in its own way, the Aldred Building on Place d'Armes, built in 1931 to test techniques for its contemporary, the Empire State Building.

"St. James St.," architect Harry Mayerovitch wrote in 1971, "has an old world, sophisticated and distinguished air. It gives a sense of intimate security by the homogeneity of its weathered stone and by its narrowness, a feeling we may never attain again because of the tyranny of the auto which demands wide open streets."

Unfortunately, St. James St., although inside the boundaries of the original old city, was excluded when Old Montreal was protected. It is thus without legal status and fair game for developers. With the financial heart of Montreal and Canada now beating elsewhere and no level of government paying attention to The Street's needs, its future is uncertain.

Movie palaces: Montreal was blessed in the first half of the 20th century with a theatre decorator named Emmanuel Briffa. The period from 1910 to the mid-1930's marked the golden years of the movie houses. It was a time when cinemas were palaces to celluloid, places where people could be fascinated not only by what they saw on the screen but by the theatres themselves.

Briffa designed the interiors of some 200 theatres in Montreal and eastern Canada, and kept this city's cinemas in the front rank of theatre design. His earliest work, in motion picture houses like the Strand (built 1912, demolished 1973) was in the older tradition of theatre design, essentially plain walls with touches of plaster decoration. But by the 1920's, Briffa had hit his stride. He filled the Palace (built in 1921 and redesigned in 1928 as Canada's first sound theatre) with Greco-Roman relief figures, windows with linen "panes," magnificent columns that looked like marble but were made of plaster (an art in itself) and—everywhere—plaster nymphs, nudes, winged serpents and figurines. The same style was repeated in other theatres, the Chateau, Rivoli, and Français among them.

Other theatre interiors were created in the "atmospheric" style—a decor meant to recall a particular setting or era. Thus the Monkland became a Moorish garden, with plaster columns, painted trees and flowers and villa walls. The Granada was the Court of Kings. The entire theatre was decorated with crests and medallions and provided with a "sky" of moving clouds and twinkling stars.

Of all this, little survives today. Many of the theatres have been demolished and in others Briffa's work has since been painted over by less imaginative decorators. The Granada is still in good condition, however, although its future is in doubt. The Rialto retains its staggering ceiling decorations of classical figures, and the Outremont's stencil designs and paintings have somehow managed to survive.

But the list goes little further. The splendor of the Palace remains only in photographs, although for the moment at least the theatre still stands. The designs of the Chateau and Rivoli survived until 1974, when the theatres were subdivided and the total impression lost.

When Briffa died in 1955, he left Montreal with a host of movie palaces as grand as any in North America. But renewal schemes in this era of high property taxes and declining movie attendance are taking their toll. The little that is left could easily go the way of the Capitol, the most lavish theatre ever built in Montreal, which was lost in 1973 at the age of 52.

Maisonneuve: Near Ontario St. and Pie IX Blvd. are some of the most unusual buildings in Montreal, located in what for 20 years (1898-1918) was the independent city of Maisonneuve.

Maisonneuve was the creation of the wealthy Dufresne brothers, Marius, Oscar and Candide, who dreamed of creating an east-end version of Westmount.

Most of the great public buildings they erected in pursuit of this dream still survive today, although few Montrealers are aware of them. There's the many-columned City Hall (1912), the magnificent market (1914), the lavish gymnasium and public bath (1914) and, on Notre-Dame St., the fire station (1914). The station is an incredible structure. Departing from the traditional classical style of the other buildings, it followed the architectural style of Frank Lloyd Wright. Sixty years later, it is still a mind-boggling sight.

Up on Sherbrooke St. at the corner of Pie IX, one of the Dufresne brothers built his mansion about 1920. The building became celebrated for its silken wallcloths and marble fireplaces and for its impressive front columns and balustrade. After serving briefly as a modern art museum in the early 1960's (with its risqué wallcloths covered with burlap) the house was sold. It is now owned by the City of Montreal which says it will be renovated for the Olympics. In the meantime, its grounds are being vandalized and its once-magnificent stained-glass windows have been boarded up.

Turn-of-the-Century Public Buildings: The City of Montreal used to build flamboyant and daring structures to house its public services. Many of these survive: the police and fire station at Laurier St. and St. Lawrence Blvd, the fire station in Point St. Charles, and the castle-like pumping station on McGregor with its turrets and towers, are a few.

Lachine: Here is one of Canada's finest collections of ancient buildings within a small area. Lining the Lachine Canal are a Hudson's Bay Company post from the early 1800's, the century-old convent of Les Soeurs de Ste-Anne and the more than 200-year-old Heaney Inn. In 1972, a British army barracks that had stood beside the inn since 1773 was demolished by the City of Lachine. But, in a reversal of policy, the city fathers announced in early 1974 that the rest of the old buildings would be preserved and the area promoted as a tourist attraction. By late 1974, however, nothing had been done.

Art Deco: This distinctive style of the 1920's and 1930's lives in Montreal in the York Theatre (interior by Briffa), the Banque

Canadienne Nationale at Metcalfe and St. Catherine, and in the Pine Ave. home of architect Ernest Cormier, who designed the main building and tower of the University of Montreal.

Mansions: Upper Westmount has become the last refuge of magnificent homes in Montreal, now that the "square mile" of downtown Montreal and the Outremont mountainside have lost their fine old mansions to high-rise development. But the Westmount mansions are increasingly costly to maintain, and even their future may be in doubt.

Religious Buildings: They're going fast but there are still some great ones in the city. Prime examples are the Grey Nuns Convent at Guy and Dorchester, built in 1871, and the Eglise du Saint Enfant Jesus in Mile End, the only church in Montreal besides Notre-Dame to be decorated by the famous religious painter Ozias Leduc.

"You can't throw a brickbat in Montreal without breaking a church window," Mark Twain observed during a visit to the city during the 19th century. But with church attendance going the same way as movie attendance, Twain's words may not hold true much longer.

The Main: St. Lawrence Blvd has lost its one-time notoriety and people are starting to notice its fine shops and distinguished commercial buildings, some of them (there's one just south of Pine) block-long arcades. The street contains numerous examples of the kind of decorative stonework that was popular in the 1880's, including the storied Monument Nationale, built a century ago as a show-case for French Canada and successively home to Jewish, Rock 'n' Roll and Theatre School traditions.

Row-Housing: Montreal is a city of renters, and this is reflected in the city's characteristic row-housing. Many of these buildings have now disappeared from the downtown area, but there are still some good districts—fancy ones around St. Louis Square and working-class homes straddling Sherbrooke St., east of St. Denis.

These areas form the most coherent sections of Montreal, but their look is a fragile thing. If one high-rise building is stuck in the middle, the appearance is destroyed.

A particularly fine bit of row-housing can be found on Baile St., in the west downtown area. This greystone block was built in the 1880's as guest houses for Lord Strathcona's mansion, which stood on nearby Dorchester Blvd. It survives today as very fine, small apartments. The block was sold in 1974 to a sub-company of Yale Properties Ltd., the development firm.

Chapter Nine

The Plight of the Mastodons

St. Joseph's Roman Catholic Church stands on a small street in Little Burgundy, just south of the CN tracks. It is a gem of a building, constructed in the 1860's and believed to have been designed by Victor Bourgeau, Montreal's leading architect in the latter half of the 19th century.

At one time, St. Joseph's was one of Montreal's richer parishes. Some 4,000 families worshipped at the church, including that of the late Governor-General Georges Vanier.

The church's interior reflects this wealth. The ceiling is decorated with fine religious paintings. There is beautiful, hand-carved woodwork and lovely statues. The parish priest, Abbé Roger Ducharme, lovingly proclaims the organ as one of the finest in Montreal.

But time has dealt harshly with St. Joseph's. The wealth of the parish has vanished, along with the era it represented. Water now leaks through the roof, damaging the paintings. The heating and electrical systems have been condemned. The building needs $300,000 worth of repairs and Abbé Ducharme hasn't the slightest idea where the money will come from.

Massive redevelopment in the area has reduced the number of families in the parish to 400. Of these, only about 10 percent practise their religion. In a church that once was regularly filled, only about 100 people show up for Sunday mass. Many of these are on welfare—too poor to make more than a token contribution to the upkeep of the building.

The collection plates that once were filled to overflowing with bills now produce only $2,000 a year in revenues. That's far less than the weekly bingo games in the church basement which bring in over $9,000 annually.

As revenues drop, costs skyrocket. Abbé Ducharme spent $23,000 to keep the church going during 1973, most of it on heating. With fuel-oil prices climbing, the costs will be even higher now.

The rotund Abbé Ducharme has been unpaid parish priest at St. Joseph's since 1969. Were it not for his determination to save the building, the church probably would have been closed and torn down by now. Even with his dedication, St. Joseph's continued existence will only be made possible by the sale of the adjoining presbytery, part of which dates from the same period as the church itself. The City of Montreal is buying the building and intends to tear it down in order to put up a modern old people's home. The sale will bring St. Joseph's about $80,000—enough to survive for another four or five years.

After that, no one knows what will happen.

"We live from day to day," says Abbé Ducharme. "It's a daily miracle."

The plight of St. Joseph's is not uncommon in Montreal. More than a dozen religious buildings have been demolished in the past five years, including some of major historical and architectural importance. Numerous others are in imminent danger of suffering the same fate.

The roll call of lost buildings includes several which any preservation-minded city would have fought to preserve.

*Chapel of Grey Nuns' Convent,
designed by Victor Bourgeau*

One of the best examples was St. Anne's Church, which was built in 1854 by John Ostell, the dominant architect in Montreal in the mid-19th century. St. Anne's, which stood near the Wellington tunnel, had the grace and style of a European chateau and was the mother church of the city's Irish-Catholic community. But it became the victim of population shifts which reduced its parish to 40 families. Despite determined efforts to save it, St. Anne's was demolished in 1970.

The same year saw the loss of the old St. Henri Church, on Place St. Henri. Built around 1890, it became the victim of redevelopment, declining attendance and mounting repair and maintenance costs—the same tendencies that threaten so many other religious buildings today. It was sold off to the Montreal Catholic School Commission for $700,000 and demolished to make way for a new school.

St. George's Roman Catholic Church was a newer building, built in the 1910-1920 period. It didn't rank as an historic structure, but it had a number of fine architectural features that would have been worth preserving. The cycle of falling revenues and rising costs caught up with it, though; it was knocked down in 1971 after experiencing a financial situation that was described as "catastrophic."

Westminster Central United Church was built during the 1880's to serve the lower Westmount area. It became a casualty of the east-west Trans-Canada autoroute when the provincial government decided to ram it through the heart of the city.

Another victim of the autoroute was the lovely old St. Anthony of Padua Church, built in 1889 to serve the Irish-Catholic community. This was a real loss—the interior of the building was finished in magnificent tones of jade green creating a striking impression of soft beauty and elegance.

The autoroute also was responsible for the 1971 demolition of Our Lady of Good Counsel Church, another Irish-Catholic house of worship. Built in 1879 in an unusual octagonal shape, it was expropriated for $400,000.

Yet another autoroute victim was the fine old Hochelaga Convent on Notre Dame St. East. Built in 1860 in the classical French style, and featuring an outstanding pillared façade and an ornate white plaster chapel, it was torn down in 1971 and replaced by an apartment complex.

The list of lost religious buildings may only be beginning, however. Without large-scale intervention by the government or the private sector, the next decade will see the disappearance of many more of Montreal's finest 19th and early 20th century churches and convents. As Abbé Claude Turmel of the Sacred Art Committee of the Montreal Archdiocese puts it: "The churches have become mastodons. Everything is in danger."

The magnificent Grey Nuns Convent at the corner of Guy and Dorchester is one of the buildings most immediately threatened. It is one of the finest examples of Victor Bourgeau's work in the city, but its continued existence is made doubtful by the recent decision to sell the building to a European development firm.

Another threatened building is Ste-Brigide Church on Dorchester, across from the new CBC building. It is a building dating from 1880, of fine architectural design. The baroque interior features Romanesque arches and slender, graceful pillars. Unfortunately, the basic quality of the design has been marred by vulgar gaudiness in the decorations—the ceiling painted in pastel pinks and blues, the altar illuminated like a carnival billboard. But despite the tasteless overlay, Ste-Brigide is a building worth preserving.

How long it will remain standing is a question, however. Demolition for Maison de Radio-Canada wiped out about 70 percent of the church's parish, and replaced family homes with a vast parking lot. More development in the area, including a $40 million complex to be called Carrefour Montreal and access roads for the east-west autoroute, will reduce the parish population still more.

The results are predictable. Three schools in the area have closed in the past four years, because of declining student population, and there are now few young people left in the district. Only 350 people show up for Sunday mass at Ste-Brigide, where five years ago there would have been 700 or 800 worshippers. Before Maison de Radio-Canada, Ste-Brigide had 3,000 families in the parish. Now there are 825.

Another lovely church just down the street, St. Pierre d'Apôtre, is in similar difficulties, thanks to the CBC. Because it is a finer church in terms of exterior architecture—a true gothic creation of Victor Bourgeau—church authorities have decided that it must be saved if possible. That makes Ste-Brigide a prime candidate for demolition, probably within five years.

Ste-Cunégonde Church in St. Henri also seems destined for the bulldozer. Built in the late French Renaissance style, Ste-Cunégonde was designed by J.O. Marchand, Montreal's leading architect in the early 20th century. Redevelopment in the area has wiped out most of its parish, and the main building has been unused for the past three years although services are still conducted in a small chapel at the back. Local residents and the parish priest are now deciding whether it will be torn down.

St. Eusèbe Church is located on Fullum St. It is a relatively new building, constructed in 1922 in a style that is characteristic of religious buildings during that period in Montreal. It doesn't rate as a masterpiece, although Abbé Turmel points out that "in 100 years it may be considered one of the best works of its time." The church's story is distressingly familiar: population in the area is declining, the building needs $200,000 worth of repairs and there is no money coming in.

The Chinese Catholic Mission in Chinatown, located in a small, 19th century building, is already on the doomed list. It is to be torn down to make way for the federal government's massive Place

Guy Favreau development. Also doomed is Notre-Dame-du-Très-Saint-Sacrement on St. Hubert St. This 1894 building with its unprepossessing exterior but classic interior is being demolished by the Pères du Saint Sacrement, who plan to replace it with a modern structure.

The greatest loss of 1974 is St. Jacques Church at the corner of St. Catherine and St. Denis. It is being demolished to make way for the construction of a mid-town campus for the University of Quebec. The steeple and south transept have been declared historical monuments by the provincial government and will be incorporated into the campus as façades. But demolition is destroying a fine basement chapel by Victor Bourgeau which the Quebec Cultural Property Commission tried in vain to have saved. Also doomed are the original exterior walls, which date back to the mid-19th century.

Preservationist groups have been fighting to save another major religious property, the Sulpician land on Sherbrooke St. West. The open spaces and fine religious buildings have become a prime target for developers and the Sulpician Order is believed to be interested in making a deal. The Cultural Property Commission recommended in December, 1972, that the entire site, which is bounded by Sherbrooke, Cedar, Guy and Atwater, be declared an historic district and preserved intact. The provincial government has never acted on the recommendation.

Roman Catholic buildings and properties aren't the only ones in danger. The largest Protestant church in Montreal—St. James United on St. Catherine St., east of The Bay—could disappear within five years.

Originally built in 1889, St. James can hold 2,000 people and was once regarded as the mother church of Methodism in Canada. But the congregation has been dwindling steadily and the talk of redeveloping the site, which has been heard on and off for the past 10 years, is now becoming serious.

The Anglican Church is seriously overdeveloped in the city center. It has four major churches standing on prime pieces of real estate: Christ Church Cathedral on St. Catherine St. between Eaton's and The Bay; St. George's across from Windsor Station; St. James the Apostle at the corner of Bishop and St. Catherine; and St. John the Evangelist, opposite Place des Arts.

"All of these churches have their problems and offers have been coming in increasingly in the past few years," admits Canon R.M. Turpin, executive officer of the Cathedral Chapter of the Diocese of Montreal. "Development projects are bringing pressure to bear on these churches, directly or indirectly."

Population shifts on Montreal Island are the main reason for the difficulties facing the downtown churches. Areas which once had a large concentration of Anglo-Celtic population, from which the Anglican Church draws most of its members, have now become mainly French Canadian or Catholic ethnic. This has left the Anglican churches increasingly isolated.

The pressures created by falling attendance and the desirability of the church sites to developers are becoming almost irresistible. There is increasing sentiment within the Anglican Church to dispose of one or more of its properties.

Were it not for fairly sizable endowments, all of the downtown Anglican churches would be money-losing operations. Even with the endowment income to offset operating losses, there is a question as to how long they can carry on.

"They are living on the resources of past generations," says Canon Turpin.

St. George's has long been considered a prime target for the developers. It stands on Dominion Square, right in the middle of the huge Canadian Pacific redevelopment tract. The Cultural Property Commission recommended in 1973 that the church be classified an historic monument, but so far nothing has been done. Canadian Pacific says it wants the church to remain, and its redevelopment plans are being drawn up on the assumption St.

George's will be preserved. But it is generally conceded within the Anglican Church that the right kind of offer could lead to the sale of the property at any time.

Whether the churches are Protestant or Catholic, the problem is fundamentally the same: Where does the money come from to maintain buildings that have outlived their original purpose?

Canon A.E. Hawes, administrative officer of the Cathedral Chapter of the Anglican Montreal Diocese, puts it this way: "If the general public wants these kept as green spaces, are they willing to do it at their expense, or only at our expense?"

Preservationists would like to see the best of Montreal's religious architecture classified as historic monuments by the provincial government. But Quebec has been notably slow to move. To date, not a single religious building in the central part of Montreal has been classified in its entirety by the provincial government.

Part of the reason for this reluctance to act is resistance from within the religious community itself. There is little financial advantage in being classified—such buildings can benefit only from a grant covering 40 percent of the cost of exterior restorations, plus a 50 percent reduction in municipal property taxes. Since churches don't pay property tax anyway, the latter concession means nothing. There is no provision for a continuing grant for the maintenance of classified buildings, which means a classified church or convent would still be left with the problem of finding enough cash to keep going on a day-to-day basis.

Apart from financial considerations, there is antipathy to any government control over church property, especially in the Sulpician Order which controls several major religious buildings in the city including Notre-Dame Church. Some individual priests also tend to resist classification, preferring to see unneeded churches torn down and replaced with more functional buildings. Curé Ben Tremblay of Ste-Catherine d'Alexandrie in the city's east end felt so strongly that a modern old people's home would be of more benefit to his parish than his 60-year-old church that he broke a bottle of champagne over the building to mark the start of demolition in 1973.

"What do 'beautiful' and 'old' mean when so many of the people in this parish are elderly and need low-cost housing," he asked at the time.

Classification can also mean the loss of millions of dollars in capital gains for a parish or a religious order. Under the law, the Quebec government has the power to intervene to stop the sale of any classified building. The sums at stake in any such situation could be considerable. The University of Quebec paid $1.5 million for St. Jacques Church. The value of the Grey Nuns Convent has been estimated as high as $15 million. The land on which Christ Church Cathedral stands is officially valued at $4.25 million and is probably worth more. The 1973 annual report of the Montreal Roman Catholic Archdiocese estimates its total holdings of land and buildings to be worth $138,723,073.

The attitude of the churches towards this wealth angers many preservationists.

Says architect Michael Fish of the Save Montreal movement: "They no longer provide services and they sit on that land. The only function they are performing is that of a speculator. The government should act to put real barriers in the way of anyone wanting to construct on church land."

Eric McLean, *Montreal Star* music critic and a pioneer in the campaign to preserve Old Montreal, goes even further. He points out that the Church has lived tax-free for centuries and suggests that religious land should revert to public ownership if it is no longer required for its original purpose.

One solution to the problem is that applied in the case of St. Jacques Church—buy the property, knock down the building and preserve the most architecturally interesting bits and pieces. The approach has the virtue of saving some of the past while eliminating large annual maintenance costs. The question is whether

Montrealers want the city's cultural heritage to be preserved in piecemeal form, rather like the ruins on the Mackenzie King estate.

Many preservationists dislike this approach, preferring if possible to keep the buildings intact. That raises the whole question of recycling—finding new uses for obsolete religious structures.

"There is no way the provincial government could afford to spend $15 million to keep the Grey Nuns Convent as a showplace," says Prof. John Bland of the McGill University School of Architecture. "But if some other use could be found for it —perhaps as government offices—then the money could be found."

A number of suggestions have been put forward for recycling Montreal's redundant religious buildings. One is for the federal and provincial governments to break away from the idea of building huge new office complexes whenever more space is needed and to look instead to the idea of converting older buildings, as is done in France and Italy. Some of the larger religious buildings in Montreal, like the Grey Nuns Convent or the Grand Seminaire on Sherbrooke St., might be well suited to such a transformation.

An even more imaginative proposal is to convert such buildings into luxury hotels. Spain's immensely successful paradors are frequently convents or monasteries which have been tastefully transformed into comfortable, romantic hotels. The same approach has never been tried in Montreal, but it is safe to say that many visitors to the city would rather stay in a modernized, properly decorated 19th century convent than in the world's largest Holiday Inn.

Buildings of the size of the Grey Nuns Convent might also be converted into old people's homes or used to provide classroom space for the city's expanding universities.

The churches themselves present a more difficult problem. In principle, both the Roman Catholic and the Anglican Church oppose having actual church buildings converted to lay purposes.

Part of this reluctance can be traced to the fate of former churches in other countries that were sold off privately when they became redundant.

"In France, there are several churches that have been converted into garages," said Abbé Turmel. "In Venice, they've put a swimming pool into a church. I don't think these are noble uses."

Proposals which preserve the dignity of unwanted churches might be considered, however. One of the most popular ideas is to use those churches best designed for the purpose for the presentation of concerts, oratorios and chorale singing. This is being done increasingly in London, Paris and New York. The crypt of St. Paul's Cathedral in London has been used for plays and television productions. Concerts are held regularly in the historic St. Germain des Pres Church in Paris and in Trinity Church on New York's Wall Street.

St. James United Church is ideally suited for this kind of use. So is Ste-Cunégonde Roman Catholic Church, which would make an ideal theatre-in-the-round.

Other proposed uses for unneeded churches are as libraries, galleries and community centers.

One successful instance of recycling an old church in Montreal is the conversion of the former Church of All Nations on Amherst Square into what is now the Quebec Sound Studio Inc.

The main hall of the church was made into two recording studios, one with a capacity of 100 musicians, the other smaller. Offices are at the back of the church.

Both the exterior and the interior of the church were kept in almost original condition. "We have no problems at all with the place," said one sound engineer. "And it's a much more interesting place to work in than some of the new buildings."

The conversion was done by André Perry, a Montreal-based record producer and promoter. "It worked out very well," he says. "It would have cost $125,000 to build a studio. We saved half of that by redoing the church."

Perry sold the studio in 1973 but still rents space in the building and does most of his recording there.

It was the attitude of the United Church of Canada that made the experiment possible. Perry stresses that not only did he encounter no opposition to his plans for the building but "they were happy to get rid of it."

Another fine example of a recycled church can be found in the 83-year-old Olivet Presbyterian Church in the heart of Toronto's Yorkville Village.

It was purchased by architect Sheldon Rosen in January, 1973. Most developers would have proceeded to reduce the red-brick, Romanesque style building to a pile of rubble, but Rosen had different ideas. Entering into a joint venture with Bovis Corporation, he undertook to transform the interior of the building into offices and galleries while retaining the original exterior, which blends handsomely with the surrounding architecture.

About $300,000 was spent installing a new heating system, new wiring, new plumbing, a small elevator, reinforcing the structure from the foundations up and putting in new floors. The result is a recycled building which is attracting international attention from architects, planners and conservationists.

A disused loft has been transformed into a bright, airy, spacious office for Rosen's firm, Group 33 Ltd. Original brickwork and wood beams have been cleaned and reinforced. Old stained-glass windows give Rosen's tastefully-furnished boardroom a striking and unique appearance.

A new floor has been added which is to serve as Canadian head office, showroom and shoe museum for Kelso Systemat Ltd. The ground floor has been used as a temporary home for part of the collection of the Ontario Art Gallery. The church basement now houses a fashionable commercial art gallery and a cosmetics boutique.

The conversion of the building from an impoverished church to economically viable offices and galleries was accomplished without one cent of public money and with no municipal tax concessions. The property was valued at $200,000 when Rosen bought it. It is now worth an estimated $1.2 million.

Rosen stresses, however, that the economic implications of this kind of recycling have to be studied carefully before a project is undertaken.

"You have to know what the rental structure is going to be," he said. "Yorkville Village is a high-rent district, a carriage-trade area. Had this building been even 300 feet from here in the wrong direction, this would just not have been feasible."

There were no complaints from the Presbyterian Church about the conversion of the building to lay purposes.

"They removed all signs from the building, had a formal deconsecration ceremony and we went ahead with their blessing," Rosen says. "The Church in this case was logical, not emotional."

Given the opportunity, Rosen would like to undertake other recycling experiments with unwanted churches. He feels some buildings might lend themselves to conversion into European-style hotels or even apartments.

"I would very much like to find a suitable project in Montreal," he says. "It has more inherent charm than Toronto."

The kind of work done by Perry and Rosen appears to hold the key to preserving many of Montreal's finest religious buildings. But, surprisingly, there has been no move on the part of church authorities to actively encourage this type of thinking, despite the alarming rate at which fine buildings are starting to disappear.

Unless some initiative comes soon, either from within the Church or from public officials, a whole epoch in Montreal's architectural history could vanish within a generation.

Chapter Ten

The Dixie Cup Syndrome

The Laurentien Hotel stands on the corner of Dorchester and Peel in the heart of downtown Montreal. Since 1948 it has been a Dominion Square landmark and a favorite stopping place for tourists visiting the city.

It's a functional building, with no particular architectural virtue. Prof. John Bland of the McGill School of Architecture calls it "cheesy." Prof. Melvin Charney of the School of Architecture of the University of Montreal dismisses it as "sixth generation art deco."

About the only architectural interest the hotel has is the fact it was used to pioneer new construction techniques after the end of the Second World War. It was the first hotel in the world to use extruded aluminum for exterior facings, and the first to make extensive use of a new finishing plastic that had just been developed in Canada and given the name Arborite. It also served as a testing ground for other new construction materials and techniques: prefabricated bathroom units, precast concrete flooring, fibreglass insulation and dry-wall partitioning.

All this plus the fact the hotel was the first to go up in North America after the war made the opening one of the major events of the period in Montreal. Newspapers of the day wrote excitedly about this new "masterpiece of architectural beauty" and described in detail the sophisticated sound system which would make the Laurentien the first hotel in Canada to bring every guest the joys of Music by Musak. Montreal Mayor Camillien Houde opened the hotel officially at a dinner on March 22, 1948, by placing a page boy's cap on the head of 16-year-old William Burke of Verdun, after which, said *The Gazette,* "Mayor Houde grasped Mr. Burke's chubby hand, chucked him under his pink chin, and dismissed him."

None of that is enough to qualify the Laurentien for protection under Quebec's 1972 Cultural Property Act. So the owners of the building, Marathon Realty, might logically assume that any plans to tear it down won't cause a ripple of public indignation in a city that allowed the Van Horne house to be destroyed. Such plans do exist and Marathon appears ready to start implementing them sometime in 1976.

The on-again, off-again saga of the Laurentien Hotel has been tantalizing Montrealers for the past year. Canadian Pacific Ltd. (which owns Marathon) plans to tear it down as part of the vast redevelopment program for the Windsor Station area. Negotiations have been going on for some time with the Bank of Montreal, which is interested in moving its head office from St. James St. to a new building to be constructed on the Laurentien site.

But when all this is going to happen remains unclear. CP Ltd. and the Bank have changed course so often on this project, that nothing seems certain any longer.

Originally it was believed that the hotel would remain open until after the Olympics. Hotel general manager Norman Boyd, an employee of Sheraton which manages the hotel for Marathon, said in an interview last March that his understanding was that the Laurentien would stay in business until Sheraton's management contract ran out at the end of 1976. As evidence of this, he cited

The Laurentien Hotel

Marathon's approval of plans for costly renovations to several hundred of the hotel's rooms.

By June, however, those plans had been changed. Charles Pike, CP Ltd's director of development, confirmed reports that the hotel would be closed earlier than 1976 and set a target date for April 11, 1975.

By September, the timetable had changed again, CP announced that the Laurentien would close its doors on Nov. 15 and started making plans for an elaborate public unveiling of the new project for the site—an unusual terraced building rising in steps away from Dominion Square.

That appeared to be the final word. Save Montreal organized a protest movement against the hotel's impending demolition, but it attracted little public support. Mr. Boyd started organizing farewell parties for the hotel staff and faithful guests as the end approached.

The bombshell came on November 7, just one week before the announced closing date. *The Montreal Star* carried a major story on its front page announcing that CP Ltd. had reversed itself yet again on the fate of the hotel. Apparently as a result of a request from the Bank of Montreal to delay the project CP abruptly decided not to close the hotel after all but to give it an 18-month stay of execution. That brought things full circle, back to the original plan to operate the hotel until after the Olympics.

CP delayed formal confirmation of *The Star's* report until after a meeting of the board of directors the following week could ratify the about-turn. But by then Mr. Boyd was already scrambling to hire new staff to replace those who had started drifting away when the original closure announcement was made.

Given CP's track record on the Laurentien, to date, it would be foolish to make any assumptions about the eventual fate of the hotel. But it does appear the company is still determined to tear it down, sooner or later. This basic decision is a cause for concern.

The Laurentien is not a beautiful building; some people go so far as to call it an eyesore. But it is a viable functioning structure which, at least until Marathon announced the hotel's closing, was making plenty of money for its owners.

The hotel has 1,004 rooms. At the time it was built, it cost $4 million to complete. A hotel of comparable size today would cost anywhere from $40 million to $65 million.

It is the last genuinely middle-class hotel in the city center; rooms are available for as little as $12 a night on special group rates. Although its occupancy rate has dropped off to an annual average of about 70 percent since the construction of new hotels in the city center, it still turns a nice profit and is always filled to near capacity during the peak summer tourist season.

To people like planner and developer Vincent Ponte, that isn't enough to warrant saving the building, however. "A building like that amortizes itself over 25 or 30 years," he says. "Then you can throw it away like a Dixie Cup. Let's face it, it is an ugly building. It was ugly even by the standards of 1948, when it was built. It fulfills a need for low-cost rooms, true, but just watch. The way this city is going, in a few years the Sheraton Mount Royal will be the Laurentien of its time. By the year 2000, the Queen Elizabeth will be a fleabag. It's all part of the way society changes. We don't build things to last anymore. We're affluent and we can afford to keep throwing things away and replacing them with newer, bigger and better."

But other experts on urban growth see the problem differently. To them, the threat to the Laurentien raises serious questions about the whole approach to land use in the city core.

Prof. R.W.G. Bryant, Co-ordinator of Urban Studies at Sir George Williams University, feels the problem of land use in the center of Montreal is much too important to be left in the hands of private enterprise.

"When you have a perfectly viable building like the Laurentien under pressure, it illustrates a general point: the need to modify the operation of the market," he says. "The social and community implications of land use, especially in urban areas, are much too important to be left to individual property owners. They must be told they have to operate within a certain social framework."

The Laurentien Hotel contains 4,000 tons of steel, 240,000 feet of copper piping, 54,000 square feet of aluminum on the exterior and one million feet of wiring. Prof. Bryant sees the destruction of the hotel as a waste of all this material and of the energy required to build a replacement structure.

"The Laurentien is not a triumph of architecture, but it is a perfectly useful building with a period of useful life left," he says. "Its destruction is completely unnecessary and not in the public interest, especially when there are plenty of parking lots around that can be built on. We talk about the energy crisis and the tremendous demand on resources of all sorts. So it becomes more and more irresponsible in our day to waste these resources. We should make it illegal to tear down perfectly good buildings purely for financial considerations, because in doing so you are wasting the general pool of energy and raw materials. The whole of our society is being geared to conservation and to stop waste. The destruction of perfectly useful buildings is just an example of a form of waste."

Michael Fish of the Save Montreal group agrees.

"The big thing is the waste of resources," he says. "How many thousand feet of river water have to be heated to cool the steel to go into the new building? Where do you dump the garbage left from the old building?"

Razing the hotel and replacing it with office space would not only remove over 1,000 low-cost hotel rooms from the city center, Fish says. It would also destroy a building that helps keep the city alive at night and replace it with one that will be empty after five o'clock.

"No one is thinking of the tourists," he says. "Most will have to take rooms that are less well located as far as the city center is concerned. If there were a business-like tourism operation in this town, they would have something to say about it.

"The city should be able to plan for a distribution of land use that takes account of all income groups. Every city wants low-cost hotels downtown, especially if they are very efficient as the Laurentien is. The city should have the right to identify these needs and enforce these uses. Any master plan for downtown would maximize the kind of space that the Laurentien Hotel rents.

"The fact that the Bank of Montreal would want to locate on Dominion Square is a pretty poor commentary on the kind of companies and individuals who run the system. It would seem they have made no study of what contribution they could make elsewhere, perhaps by giving a new square to the city."

Fish also points out another social consequence: the razing of the Laurentien Hotel will mean the loss of about 250 permanent hotel staff jobs, with resulting dislocation. Also lost will be the 100 summer season jobs that are taken mainly by students and the 85 to 100 jobs with Murray's, which handles all catering at the hotel.

"The Bank of Montreal's economists don't figure that when they are calculating profits," he says.

One of the problems facing buildings like the Laurentien is that, while they may still be economically viable, there is a tax incentive in tearing them down and building something new.

Once a building's original value has been fully depreciated, a company can no longer use it as a corporate income tax deduction. Even though the building's market value may have increased over the years, its book value for tax deduction purposes is zero.

That often makes it profitable for a company to raze it and to rebuild on the site, thereby creating a new tax deduction.

"The depreciation system where corporate taxes are concerned mitigates for the most wasteful use of resources possible," says Fish. "There is a great premium on new building activity. There should be some reward for conservation. As it is, anyone who conserves and maintains a property is penalized by the tax laws in comparison with his wasteful neighbor. Big business knows this very well."

Meanwhile, back at the Laurentien, Mr. Boyd is trying to cope with the problem of engaging and holding staff for a hotel that is still facing almost certain demolition. It's not easy.

Boyd is a Saskatchewan native who was hired by the hotel as a room clerk when it first opened back in 1948. He worked his way up to general manager the hard way. Now he finds old-timers on his staff leaving and a reluctance on the part of new people to take jobs with an operation that will be closing down within a year.

For him, the prospect of the Laurentien being destroyed is painful. It's been the center of his life for more than 25 years, and he finds it hard to imagine what mid-town Montreal will be like without it.

"I came out of the Air Force in 1946 and came to Montreal," he recalls. "They had a little shack on the corner here where they were hiring staff for the hotel that was about to be built. I went in and they took me on.

"If they tear it down before I retire, I may become the only man in North America who has been with a hotel from the time of its inception to the time of its demolition."

Chapter Eleven

The Compromised Commission

Old Montreal is a camera-bug's paradise. The narrow streets, the cobblestones, the fine 18th and 19th century buildings and the old-fashioned street lamps all combine to evoke the nostalgia of another time.

In the summer, the area around Jacques Cartier Square is crowded with Montrealers and tourists. They come to enjoy the atmosphere, to shop in the boutiques and flower stalls and to sample the many fine restaurants which have established themselves in the old quarter.

On the surface, Old Montreal would appear to be one of the great success stories of the Drapeau administration, and in some ways it is. Less than 15 years ago, the area seemed headed for mass demolition and total redevelopment. Today, it is one of the great attractions of Montreal.

But many of those most familiar with Old Montreal—the people who live there—are not happy with everything the city administration has done. As one somewhat bitter property owner puts it: "If Drapeau is the father of Old Montreal, he's the father of a handicapped child."

The designation of Old Montreal as an historic district in the early 1960's imposed some severe restrictions on property owners in the area. But the objections aren't about that. Rather, they are over the direction—or, more properly, the lack of direction —which the city has given to the old quarter over the past decade.

"It's like a seed that was planted and then never tended," says one Old Montreal resident. "The city put in some picture postcard views for the tourists and then let the whole thing drop."

No one disputes the need to preserve an area as rich in architecture and historical associations as Old Montreal. The old quarter is important not just for its intrinsic value, but for the variety and sense of tradition it gives to the city.

"But Old Montreal must become part of the fabric of the city," says music critic Eric McLean, the man who spearheaded the campaign to preserve Old Montreal. "It cannot just be a museum quarter like Upper Canada Village."

The way to keep Old Montreal alive is with people—not tourists who wander in for a few hours, but people who work, play and live in the old section, thereby bringing it to life.

Urban planner H.P Daniel van Ginkel recognized that when he drew up the city's original plan for the development of Old Montreal. His proposals called for large-scale renovation of existing buildings into housing and for "in-fill" construction of homes in the parking lots. But the plan was modified over time. Any housing in Old Montreal today exists because private citizens were willing to put up thousands of dollars to renovate dilapidated structures into comfortable living quarters.

"The city has allowed the old quarter to become too specialized," says McLean. "You've got boutiques and discothèques. But there are few or no schools, parks, grocery stores or laundromats."

Says van Ginkel: "We warned the city not to make another Coney Island out of it. Unfortunately, that's exactly what happened."

*The Papineau house in Old Montreal,
restored by Eric McLean*

The drive to save Old Montreal dates from Eric McLean's purchase of the old Papineau house in 1961. The historic 18th century building was in deplorable condition and was being used as a flop house for drunks and down-and-outs. McLean bought the building against the advice of just about everyone.

"People thought I had taken leave of my senses," he recalls. "They told me not to do it, the area was dirty, rat-infested and was all going to be knocked down anyway."

McLean went ahead anyway, pouring $250,000 into restoration work, mostly during the 1961-1967 period. The old flop house became a showpiece, and restoring buildings in Old Montreal suddenly became a fashionable thing to do.

The excitement caused by McLean's work and concern generated by a developer's plan to raze a large section of the old city for a parking lot prompted civic authorities to make their first moves towards preserving the district. But, characteristically as it turned out, the first move to save Old Montreal was a compromise.

The original plan for Old Montreal was to protect the entire area that had been enclosed by the fortifications that surrounded the city from about 1720 to 1820. Had that plan been followed, the preservation area would have extended over about 135 acres. In fact, it covers less than 100 acres.

The north wall of the old city stood between the present St. James St. and Fortification Lane. But the legal boundary of Old Montreal extends only to the south side of Notre Dame St. As a result, three important street-sides, including architecturally imposing St. James St., have been left unprotected. The reason for this strange decision appears to have been politics, pure and simple.

"I think they realized that if they were to include all the area within the 1723 wall, they would have to curtail construction of the Palais de Justice (for which the province was then demolishing buildings) and the Banque Canadienne Nationale on Place d'Armes," says John King, curator of the Chateau de Ramezay and a member of the Viger Commission. "They could not have reconciled their plans with these two buildings, so they changed the boundaries."

Once the precinct of Old Montreal was established, the city immediately invested about $6 million in improvements. The 1845 Bonsecours Market was given a magnificent face-lifting and renovated so as to accommodate municipal offices. Cobblestones were laid on St. Paul St. and Jacques Cartier Square and 19th century-style street lights put up.

"The cobblestones and the street lamps were to be the first phase of improvements in Old Montreal," McLean says. "So far, they're the only phase. The city hasn't put a nickel into Old Montreal since 1966 and I'm terrified they're not going to do anything until after the Olympics."

Even the limited steps taken so far are somewhat tainted, McLean feels.

"The city might have been showing some concern for its heritage, but its primary interest was in finding a solution to an area where property values were falling faster than anywhere in the city—with an equivalent loss in tax revenues," he says.

"If it had been economically feasible, they wouldn't have hesitated to tear down the entire quarter, the Chateau de Ramezay included, and put in high-rise towers."

As it turned out, things didn't happen that way—quite the opposite. Acting with the provincial government, the City of Montreal established a 21-member watchdog group called the Viger Commission, named for Montreal's first mayor (1833). Architects, planners, historians and other citizens were, and are, included on the body.

The Commission's immediate mandate was to oversee the development of Old Montreal. But it was also given a larger function: to advise the civic administration on historic buildings throughout the city.

The Viger Commission's record in the old quarter is admirable. Although much needs to be done, the old city has been preserved and several plans that would have compromised the character of Old Montreal, including an expressway along the river front, have been sidetracked largely through the Commission's efforts.

But outside the old city, there has been little to suggest that an historical advisory committee even exists in Montreal. This is not because Viger Commission members are incompetent—they are a knowledgeable, dedicated group. Nor is it because they don't give advice—they give it freely.

The problem is, as McLean puts it: "We can make recommendations until we're blue in the face. But it's up to Quebec whether something is saved or not."

The provincial government, for its part, has not been in a noticeable hurry to save historic buildings from demolition through the procedure of classification.

Montreal might learn a lesson here from Toronto. A 1967 Ontario law gave that city the right to designate historic buildings, a power Montreal does not yet have. But no buildings were so designated until 1972 when the preservation-minded Crombie administration took control of Toronto City Hall. Since then, the Toronto Historical Board has recommended that about 700 buildings be designated. Not one has been turned down by City Council.

Like the Toronto Historical Board, the Viger Commission has no real powers. It must depend on a positive attitude within City Council to achieve anything. Significantly, the Commission does not report directly to the Council, or even to the mayor's office. It reports to the City Planning Department, which in turn forwards its recommendations to the administration.

"This is effective only if the planners are sympathetic," says McLean. "It would be more effective if the Viger Commission could report directly to the public, so people could see how our recommendations are being ignored by the city."

The problem is compounded, McLean adds, because "though the city has a very good planning department, it regards it as a frill—not as persons of superior authority in that domain."

Understandably, the end result is a good deal of frustration.

"It would be all right to be on a Commission if we knew we were understood and our advice followed," says one member, architect Claude Beaulieu.

The stagnation now evident in Old Montreal is not due to a lack of ideas. In 1965, the City Planning Department drew up a set of impressive plans for the quarter. Several parks were to be created, one of them on the site of the present parking lot between the Chateau de Ramezay and Rasco's Hotel. The Champ de Mars, now also a parking lot, was to be completely done over, with gardens and excavations of the old walls still buried there. Parking garages would be built around the old quarter to cut down traffic flow through the area. Some streets would be turned into pedestrian malls. There would be a river garden down from Place d'Youville.

On paper, the project looked fine. In practice, nothing has been done to implement it. The city insists the plans have not been abandoned but in the meantime there are city-owned buildings in the old quarter, like the 140-year-old Rasco's Hotel, that are rapidly deteriorating. Equally serious, there are residents and businessmen in the old city who are suffering because of the inaction.

"The city says it is not in real estate," says McLean. "But they got into it when they classified the area. They're unfair to the proprietors in the sense that they classified the area and then do nothing to encourage improvement in it."

The city administration's strangely ambivalent attitude towards encouraging restoration work in Old Montreal is a frequent topic among critics of the way the quarter has been handled.

"There are many empty buildings there now, and they're frighteningly expensive to restore," says van Ginkel. "It is a problem but you can do many things by means of tax incentives. Everywhere in the world there are examples of temporary lower taxes when people repair buildings. The city could encourage residents to move in and small businesses to return by this means."

In fact, the city has provision in its laws both for renovation subsidies and for tax concessions. But the way in which they've been applied has caused a great deal of unhappiness.

One man who undertook the restoration of an old house in the quarter said he was promised by the city that his taxes would be frozen as a concession for undertaking the work. The pledge was not only ignored after the work was completed, but the city actually increased his assessment dramatically. The same person had no better luck with the provincial government, which reneged on a promise to pay part of the cost of restoring the exterior of his two-centuries-old house.

Another Old Montreal resident reported that his hopes for a rebate on restoration expenditures were smashed when the province instituted a cut-off date. Work done prior to that date, as his was, was declared not eligible for assistance.

The owners of the Brasserie des Fortifications, just off Jacques Cartier Square, did a fine and costly renovation job on their premises, including the constructing of eight apartments. They were shocked at the city's attitude after they had finished.

"They passed a by-law in 1969 saying they would give 20 percent or 25 percent subsidies to renovation projects in Old Montreal," one of the owners said. "We followed the Viger Commission; we did what we were supposed to do, but when we brought our application for a subsidy to City Hall they laughed at us and said they had no money. They voted $100,000 for those subsidies. Where did that money go?"

The owners added that their tax assessment, which they thought was frozen, went up five times its original figure when renovations were completed.

"We found a section of the old city walls in the basement," one said. "They told us to dig it out and they would pay us. So we dug it out, through all the sand because it's where the river front used to be. Then the city said: 'The province will pay you.' The province said: 'We have no money.'

"You know, some people think it's a gold mine down here. And in the summer, with the tourists, it's O.K. But in the winter, it's very hard to be in business here. There are a lot of failures down here because they haven't had the boost from the city they should have had.

"With the city it's all talk, talk, talk and no action. The mayor could have put his restaurant in Rasco's Hotel, but he put it in the Windsor instead."

If the residents and businessmen in the old quarter are disturbed, so are the members of the Viger Commission. Their dissatisfaction began with the original undersized boundaries of the old city.

"The problem was that legislation setting up the Viger Commission came before legislation setting aside the old city," says van Ginkel. "This to me was an absolute disaster."

"But what could we do?" asks John King of the 269-year-old Chateau de Ramezay. "We are continually trying to get the boundaries extended, particularly to include St. James St. where there are some very fine pieces of architecture."

Commission members tend to acknowledge their weakness, but they bridle at suggestions they do nothing.

"Our recommendations on demolition in the old quarter are followed," says McLean. "It annoys me when people say we do nothing. We stopped the autoroute along Commissioners St., which would have completely destroyed the waterfront. And it was on our recommendation that the city put up the reproductions of 19th century street lamps. We also got the provincial government to put only a two-storey frontage on the Notre Dame St. side of the Palais de Justice. They had a much taller building planned."

But other recommendations from the Viger Commission have met with less success.

"We've long recommended the establishment of a bureau of professionals concerned exclusively with Old Montreal to serve as a repository for documents about the old city," McLean said. "It would be an information center for people interested in investing in Old Montreal. They can't go anywhere now. Such a bureau would cost $60,000 a year and the return would be limitless."

John King stressed another aspect of the Commission's weakness: "In Old Montreal we do whatever we can to try and maintain the architectural appearance. But we can only really control the exterior appearance of buildings. Even in the case of demolition, we can only make recommendations. We have no actual powers. It's frustrating because we feel that, as students of Old Montreal, all this is sometimes for naught. We feel, as a body, that we are an authority on the place and we feel frustrated when our recommendations can go only so far."

Commission member Judge Kenneth Mackay offered this example of frustration: "There's a deplorable sign on Notre Dame St. for Joe's Steak House. In July, 1973, I wrote a letter for the Commission to the city pointing out that the sign is not in character with Old Montreal. The city can control signs in the old city but a year later the sign is still there. All that's happened is that somebody came out and painted 'temporary sign' on it."

If the Commission members are frustrated with the administration's actions over Old Montreal, they feel at a total loss when it comes to protecting the historical character of the city as a whole.

They have made recommendations to preserve buildings like the Van Horne house and Windsor Station. But for all the action they received, they might as well have saved their breath. The recommendations they make carry little more weight than those coming from private individuals.

"The Viger Commission was originally conceived as having more power," says Judge Mackay. "I objected at the time to the restriction of power because I foresaw the difficulties. We can't deal with things directly as similar committees can in New Orleans or Philadelphia. They can stop demolition, we can't.

"We on the Commission can see what's happening here and we can see what's happening in other cities. And we get very frustrated because a lot could be done, should be done, and is not. You know, in Philadelphia they are preserving buildings under expressways. They realize that someday the expressway will be no good, and they'll still have their little Queen Anne house underneath."

John King echoes the sentiment: "We'd like more authority, we'd like to be a more important body than we are. And I think the citizens in general would like more authority in the area of old buildings placed in our hands. In most places where old buildings and areas are preserved, there are committees that have the authority to stop demolition. In New Orleans, if a committee member sees something valuable being torn down he can stop it then and there until there is a decision on the value of the building. But the Jacques Viger Commission is simply an advisory body."

Members of the Viger Commission expressed bitter disappointment over the demolition of the Van Horne house in September, 1973. They were particularly distressed because both they and the provincial Cultural Property Commission had recommended the building's preservation.

After the fight was lost, Judge Mackay sent a letter to the then Minister of Cultural Affairs, Dr. François Cloutier, deploring the loss. In it he emphasized that the house had been crucial to the character of Montreal and stressed the need of a city for buildings of all ages.

Dr. Cloutier never answered the letter.

"The Commission does good work," says architect Beaulieu. "But it's a bad instrument. We miss half of what we should do."

Commission members agree there are many areas in Montreal that should be protected, apart from the old quarter. Most frequently mentioned are Crescent St., St. Louis Square and Dorchester Blvd. west of Atwater. But no one is optimistic that the Commission's powers will be extended to give them a firmer mandate in the protection process.

Despite this, the Commission's success in maintaining Old Montreal is undeniable.

"I think we've been successful in keeping out the people whose idea of restoration is barnwood and a sign in gothic letters," says Beaulieu.

Hopefully, sooner or later, the next phase will be implemented and Old Montreal will get the housing and other amenities it needs to be fully integrated into the fabric of Montreal society. Until then, at least the old buildings are still standing, waiting.

Chapter Twelve

Lethargy in Quebec City

Apathy and inaction by the Quebec Liberal government of Premier Robert Bourassa have been important contributing factors to the recent destruction of several outstanding buildings in Montreal. Despite being handed broad powers by the Cultural Property Act of 1972, the government has chosen to look the other way while developers cut swaths through some of the city's finest old districts.

When the legislation was passed in July, 1972, the Minister of Cultural Affairs at the time, Claire Kirkland-Casgrain, called it one of the most outstanding measures of its kind in the world.

The bill gave the government sweeping and sometimes controversial powers. But the minister claimed they were necessary to protect all aspects of Quebec's heritage, from primitive artifacts to fine art.

The law has now been on the statute books for over two years. On the basis of Montreal's experience in that time, it is obvious the legislation is failing in one of its main aims: to save buildings of historical or architectural interest from demolition.

Since the act was passed, Montreal has lost several important structures that deserved to be preserved. The Van Horne house on Sherbrooke St. was a classic example of the government's failure to move, despite repeated urgings from its own experts. Other losses include: the Capitol Theatre, the Killam house at Stanley and Sherbrooke, Saxonhurst on Redpath St., the fine row of Victorian houses at Dorchester and St. Mathieu and the Balmoral Hotel on Notre Dame St.

In more or less imminent danger are the Grey Nuns Convent, the streetscape of St. Denis St., and many of the old banks on St. James St.

The provincial government seems prepared to stand by and let it all happen.

The Cultural Property Act allows the government to "recognize" or "classify" buildings and areas of historic and architectural importance, "the conservation of which is in the public interest."

A recognized building has limited protection. It may not be demolished, altered, sold or changed without 30 days notice to the minister. But after the 30 days have expired, anything can be done to it.

A classified building is provided with stronger safeguards. It cannot be altered or demolished without written consent from the minister, who must first obtain the advice of appointed experts. The owner of any classified building not used commercially is eligible for a 50 percent reduction in municipal taxes and for grants for exterior restoration.

The act also provided for the creation of a 12-member body, to be known as the Cultural Property Commission. The Commission was to "give its advice to the Minister on any question referred to it by him" and to "make recommendations to the Minister on any matter relating to the conservation of cultural property."

In October, 1972, the government announced the appointment as Commission chairman of Georges-Emile Lapalme, a former leader of the Quebec Liberal Party and Minister of Cultural Affairs in the cabinet of Jean Lesage. His salary was fixed at $25,000 a year. Other members of the Commission were chosen to represent a wide range of historic and artistic disciplines including architec-

The Mondat house... once classified, now destroyed

ture, fine arts, antique furniture, archeology and letters The first meeting of the new body took place in Quebec City on Nov. 4, 1972.

The mandate of the Commission was to act as the guardian of Quebec's historic and artistic heritage. That was the theory anyway. The reality was much different—the Commission became a toothless watchdog, held on a very short chain. Occasionally, it has delivered a loud bark, but no one in Quebec City has paid much attention.

Some of its recommendations have been collecting dust on the desk of the Minister of Cultural Affairs for two years. Others have been flatly rejected.

The Commission has been given no budget of its own, which means it has no resources to hire expert technical staff to assist it in its work. Nor has it been given any authority—all the decision-making power remains vested in the minister. The Commission is confined to recommending and protesting.

If the government were deeply committed to the cause of preserving Quebec's cultural heritage, none of this would cause grave concern. But the Bourassa administration has shown no such commitment.

The quality of the Commission members themselves has never been called into question. Almost all have national or international reputations as experts in their fields. Their commitment to preserving the best of Quebec's cultural heritage, from archeological finds to important buildings, is absolute.

"The Commission is serious-minded, with affirmative intentions," says member David Carter. "We have seen the problems and we are all looking for better answers."

Some of the answers the Commission has proposed could be of extreme importance for the future course of Montreal's development. Montreal is the richest city in Canada in terms of historic buildings worth preserving and the Commission has recognized this. But the government has been dragging its feet in taking the kind of action the Commission would like to see.

On the entire Island of Montreal, only about 30 buildings have been recognized or classified by the Quebec government since the Cultural Property Act was passed. In contrast, Toronto's preservation-minded city council, in office less than two years, approved 750 buildings in that city to be officially designated as being of historical or architectural importance. New York City's Landmarks Commission has designated almost 400 buildings as being worth preserving.

Quebec's reluctance to use the powers contained in the Cultural Property Act can be traced to two sources: the absolute power vested in the minister by the law and the low priority given by the provincial government to cultural heritage preservation.

The dangers of absolute ministerial authority became clear in the Van Horne house case. The building was allowed to be reduced to rubble because the minister at that time, Dr. François Cloutier, chose to ignore loud and public protests of the Commission and of several of his own key advisors.

The incident illustrated the kind of treatment the Commission has received from the government since its creation. It led to the tempers of Commission members boiling over in public.

"The time allowed was too short to permit those who wanted to save the house to explore solutions," David Carter said later. "The dimension of the loss still hasn't sunk in on many people."

The reasons why Dr. Cloutier and Premier Bourassa allowed the Van Horne house to be destroyed have never been made clear. But the way in which the Cultural Affairs Minister arbitrarily opted to ignore the advice and protests of the Cultural Property Commission indicates the inability of the members to influence events.

The provincial government's casual attitude towards preservation was further demonstrated in the case of a small farmhouse just outside Brossard, on the south shore of the St. Lawrence River from Montreal.

The building was an old French-Canadian stone dwelling, built in 1789. It was known as the Maison Mondat and was located at 5695 Lapinière in Brossard, just off the Eastern Townships autoroute.

In 1966, the house was expropriated by the provincial Roads Department, which intended to put a new four-lane highway through the site. As often happens in expropriations of this kind, actual work on the highway was not expected to begin for several years. In the meantime, the Mondat family—father Pierre and son Euclide—were allowed to continue living in the house.

According to Euclide Mondat, the family remained in occupancy until December, 1972. At that time they were forced by the

Transport Department to leave (which in the interim had absorbed the old Roads Department), on the grounds that construction of the highway would soon begin. Mondat says that when the family left, the little stone farmhouse was in good condition.

In the meantime, efforts were being made to have the building classified as an historic monument, thereby protecting it against the impending demolition. Chairman Lapalme of the Cultural Property Commission won't give any details of the case or reveal who requested the classification, but the record shows that during its meeting of May 3-5, 1973, the Commission approved a recommendation calling on the Cultural Affairs Minister to proceed with classification.

In this case, the minister followed the recommendation. Notice of intention to classify the building was delivered to the Transport Department on Nov. 2, 1973. The house was formally registered as an historic monument six days later and given a registration number: 115259. Notification of the classification was published in the Quebec Official Gazette on Jan. 9, 1974.

That should have been the end of the story. By classifying the building, the Cultural Affairs Minister should have stopped any plans to knock down the old farmhouse so a highway could be pushed through. The Transport Department should have been sent back to the drawing board to look for an alternate route.

Unfortunately, it didn't work out that way.

The Transport Department went back to Cultural Affairs and asked that the building be declassified on the grounds it had been so damaged by vandalism as to constitute a "public danger." Astoundingly, the Cultural Affairs Department agreed.

"The house has been abandoned and a great deal of damage has been done," said Jean-Guy Theoret, head of the department's Historic Sites and Monuments branch, in an effort to rationalize the decision. "It would cost a fortune to restore the building. If it were an extraordinary house it might be worthwhile, but there are others of the same generation in the immediate area. The money would be better spent elsewhere."

Theoret blamed the whole problem on the lack of staff in his department. If the house had been studied more thoroughly when the original proposal came through, classification never would have taken place, he contends.

But the rationale leaves something to be desired. For instance, the reason the house fell into disrepair was because the Transport Department ordered the Mondat family out and then let the building stand vacant, making it easy prey for vandals.

According to section 30 of the Cultural Property Act, "every classified cultural property must be kept in good condition." That placed the responsibility for maintaining the Maison Mondat in good shape on the owner of the property, the Transport Department.

Instead of enforcing this section of the act, the Cultural Affairs Department allowed the Transport Department to use the claim that the building was in bad condition as an excuse to declassify and demolish. That is exactly what happened; declassification took place in June, 1974, and in July, the house was destroyed by fire.

The moral for any other owner who wants to get rid of a classified building seems clear: let it stand vacant for a year and allow the vandals to have a go at it. Then apply to the Cultural Affairs Department for declassification on the grounds of "public danger," citing the Maison Mondat case as a precedent.

The Maison Mondat isn't the only example of an historic building coming under pressure from the government. A house known as the Maison Gosselin at Ange-Gardien was demolished by Hydro-Quebec in 1973 after the Cultural Property Commission had recommended it be classified.

In its 1972-1973 annual report, the Commission commented: "In the past, government bodies (federal, provincial, municipal) were the great destroyers of heritage buildings. Public Works destroyed numerous historic buildings, the Roads Department tore apart districts and villages of historic interest, Hydro-Quebec by-passed the law protecting Ile d'Orléans...

"The Commission recommends that the Cultural Affairs Department have the entire supervision of cultural heritage. This can only be done through interministerial agreement."

So far, the only interministerial agreement has been to allow the Transport Department to destroy yet another historic building.

Quebec's current Minister of Cultural Affairs is a 39-year-old MNA from Terrebonne named Denis Hardy. He succeeded Dr. Cloutier in the post in the fall of 1973 and has maintained a low profile ever since. His main problem is obvious, however, even if he doesn't talk publicly about it: his department is being starved for cash by a government which is not prepared to put up the money to implement its own legislation.

Provincial government estimates for the 1973-1974 fiscal year showed that spending on cultural affairs totalled just over $21 million. Only four departments of the Quebec government get less money. Of that $21 million, most was spent on staff salaries and the performing arts. Only $4.6 million was allocated for the preservation of historical and archaeological sites and properties. Of that, $2 million came from the federal government's $8.5 million program to restore Quebec City's Place Royale.

This means Quebec's net spending in 1973-1974 on preserving historic buildings was only $2.6 million. In comparison, the 1973 provincial government grant to keep Man and His World going was $4.5 million, with the City of Montreal kicking in another $2 million. More than anything else, those figures show where the priorities lie.

The federal government is spending as much as the province on restoring and preserving cultural heritage in Quebec. Tourist-oriented cultural investments under programs sponsored by the Department of Regional Economic Expansion involve over $13.3 million in federal spending over the 1970-1975 period.

"The Quebec government is very largely dependent on federal handouts for the preservation of its cultural heritage," admitted an official of the Cultural Affairs Department. "Many people don't realize that restoration projects like Place Royale and the Oka chapel are being done with federal funds. It is only possible to save many of Quebec's cultural areas with federal government help."

The cash starvation suffered by the Quebec Cultural Affairs Department extends beyond preserving historic buildings, however. As Mr. Theoret indicated, the department is badly understaffed, largely because no money is available to hire the expert personnel needed.

Section 52 of the Cultural Property Act requires that the minister arrange for a complete inventory of all cultural property in the province that might be recognized or classified. But a department official admitted it would be decades, if ever, before that section of the law is complied with because there is no money available for the work.

Worthwhile projects have to be turned down because of lack of funds. When a McGill group proposed doing an inventory of Montreal's religious buildings that would have cost the government only $30,000, the idea had to be rejected because of budget.

Under the law, the government has the right of first refusal on any recognized property over 50 years old that is put up for sale. In reality it is a hollow power because there are no funds for this purpose.

"Even if the Van Horne house had been classified, it could not have been purchased by the Quebec government under this right of preemption because there isn't $800,000 in Quebec City for such a purpose," said Mr. Lapalme.

Funds to provide grants for restoration or repair work on classified buildings are extremely limited. The annual report of the Cultural Affairs Department for 1972-1973 notes that $727,622.27 was given out for this purpose during the year.

What it doesn't say is that the largest single grant, $586,000 for work on the Quebec Seminary, was federal government money. The Quebec government's total contribution to restoring historic buildings in 1972-1973 was a paltry $139,622.27.

The low budgetary priority given the department by the provincial government means that, in practical terms, the Cultural Property Act is almost powerless to preserve Quebec's heritage.

"The law seems to have been written more or less in the abstract," David Carter says. "It is based on principles that may be valid in other countries like Mexico and France, which have rich archaeological treasures. But the Quebec situation is much different. The government did not consult in practical terms with those people and groups directly concerned with preservation."

Mr. Lapalme estimates that the budget of the Cultural Affairs Department would have to be tripled before it could effectively carry out the powers given it by legislation. There is no sign that this kind of money is anywhere on the horizon. Commented one expert on historical preservation: "I talked privately to a cabinet minister about the problem recently. He just shrugged."

The money shortage is a key reason why so many of the recommendations from the Cultural Property Commission have been ignored by the government. For instance, during its meeting of May 3-5, 1973, the Commission adopted a resolution recommending the classification of Windsor Station as an historic monument "in view of the exceptional interest it represents from an historic, architectural and urban point of view." That was well over a year ago. To date, nothing has been done.

The reason for the government's inaction isn't hard to find. Windsor Station is at the center of a multi-million dollar redevelopment program which Canadian Pacific Ltd. is planning for the downtown area. By classifying Windsor Station, the government would be prohibiting demolition of the building or any alteration to it.

That would amount to direct intervention in a scheme involving millions of dollars in construction spending and increased property tax revenues for the City of Montreal. That immediately makes the whole issue a political hot potato and goes a long way towards explaining why the Commission's recommendation has been on the minister's desk for so long. Classification of Windsor Station might well mean demands from Canadian Pacific for government compensation. Quebec does not have that kind of money to spend.

Other recommendations with important implications for the development of Montreal have also been shelved by the minister, apparently for the same combination of political and financial considerations.

For instance, a proposal was passed at the Commission's meeting of December 1-2, 1972, that the Sulpician property on Sherbrooke St. be declared an historic district, thus giving it the same degree of protection that Old Montreal enjoys.

At the meeting of February 22-23, 1973, a proposal to classify the Mount Stephen Club on Drummond St. was approved. The federal government has already recognized the ornate Victorian building with its 22-carat gold doorknobs as being of national architectural and historic importance and intends to put up a plaque. But only provincial government classification can protect the building.

During the May 3-5, 1973, meeting, the Commission approved a recommendation that the Victor Bourgeau chapel in St. Jacques Church be classified "because of its historical and architectural interest." At the same meeting, motions were approved to classify St. George's Anglican Church on Dominion Square and the Grey Nuns Convent on Dorchester Blvd.

None of these recommendations has been acted on. The official explanation from the government is that it is easy to pass a recommendation, but very difficult to implement it.

"It is a matter of finding money, and of finding a useful purpose for a building," says Lorenzo Paré, chief information officer for the

149

Cultural Affairs Department. There are some very important projects in mind for the buildings but they involve a lot of money and negotiations are still going on. I can't say any more about them than that."

What it boils down to is that the government has established a set of criteria for preserving historic buildings that is completely divorced from the provisions of the Cultural Property Act. To be worthy of classification, a building must: a. be made to serve a functional purpose, and b. be economically viable and not constitute any drain on government resources. The mere fact that a building is intrinsically worth preserving for itself does not appear to be a major consideration.

The cases of the Van Horne house and the Shaughnessy mansion on Dorchester Blvd. West illustrate how these criteria are applied.

The Van Horne house perished because no one was given a chance to propose a viable alternative use for it that would have bailed the government out. The Shaughnessy house survived and was classified because a useful purpose for it was found.

The Shaughnessy house was built between 1876 and 1877 and is regarded as a fine example of pure Victorian architecture. It was designed by William T. Thomas, one of the finest Canadian architects of the period, and the man who built the Mount Stephen Club and St. George's Church. The house had important historical connections. It was lived in for a time by Sir William Van Horne, and later by Lord Shaughnessy, president of the CPR at the turn of the century.

The building had been owned by the Sisters of Service, a Toronto-based order of nuns, since 1934. They had run it as a hostel for working girls and students.

In 1973, they decided to close the hostel and dispose of the property. An option on the site was taken out in April of that year by architect Ian Martin, who planned to demolish the mansion and ultimately to construct a high-rise building on the land. His option to purchase was conditional on being allowed to tear down the existing structure.

When preservationist groups learned of Martin's intentions, the battle was joined and a campaign launched to persuade the provincial government to classify the building. The Save the Mansion cause was reinforced by a telegram sent September 12, 1973, to James MacLellan, one of the leaders in the fight to preserve the Van Horne house, by P.H. Bennett, secretary of the National Historic Sites and Monuments Board in Ottawa. In the telegram, Bennett said the Board had studied the Shaughnessy mansion and had reached the conclusion that it was a building "of national architectural and historical importance."

Even with this kind of prodding, the provincial government dragged its heels on classification. A great deal of political manoeuvering was taking place in the background, but the fundamental problem, it appears, was finding a viable alternative solution that would keep the building intact.

It was only after a wealthy Montrealer, Phyllis Bronfman Lambert, actually bought the property outright for $725,000 and a team of experts proved that the building could be put to profitable use with no financial obligation or investment by the provincial government that classification was approved in February, 1974. It now appears the mansion will be restored to its former glory and used for public rooms for a new apartment hotel to be constructed behind it.

This insistence on viability is one of the main reasons for holding off classification of other important buildings in the Montreal area. It is also proving to be one of the main sources of frustration among members of the Cultural Property Commission. In this situation, Commission chairman Lapalme becomes the man in the middle.

Lapalme is basically a political person, who tends to be guarded when talking about the Commission's problems and its difficulties with the government.

"The Commission is purely an organism of consultation," he says. "In a sense, we act as the minister's lawyers."

But he finds it difficult to conceal his dissatisfaction with the Commission's complete lack of authority. He notes pointedly that the old Historic Monuments Commission, the predecessor of the present body, had much more freedom of action.

"The Historic Monuments Commission had powers we would like to have," he says.

Lapalme carefully avoids direct criticism of the government. But his unhappiness with the Commission's lack of funds is also apparent.

"We have no budget, and that's the story," he says. "We do not even have any money to hire researchers."

The salaries of Lapalme and his secretary and the honorariums paid to Commission members ($100 a day for the meetings they attend) come directly from the Cultural Affairs Department's Service de Patrimoine. There are no other funds for the Commission. This means the Commission has no support staff to provide technical information—all such work has to be turned back to experts within the department, who are already badly overworked.

The lack of funds combines with the cavalier treatment of recommendations to frustrate the commissioners. The failure of the minister to act and the outright rejection of some proposals led Commission members to approve a resolution in May, 1973, calling for decisions on all recommendations "with the briefest possible delay." The Commission also asked the minister to provide explanations in cases where recommendations were rejected.

Lapalme says the situation has improved since the resolution was passed, but recommendations still wait months and even years for ministerial action.

Given a highly motivated minister and adequate funds with which to work, the Commission could be performing an important role in directing the pattern of development in Montreal by ensuring that the most important historic and architecturally-interesting buildings are preserved.

Under existing circumstances, however, its impact on the course of development in Montreal is marginal at best.

Chapter Thirteen

Ottawa's Split Personality

The federal government shows a split personality in its dealings with Montreal.

On one side is Ottawa the conservationist, pouring money into restoration work through DREE projects, using the National Historic Sites and Monuments Board to pinpoint buildings worth saving, and creating a new national body, Heritage Canada, to watch over the country's cultural riches.

On the other side is Ottawa the destroyer, wiping out a huge neighborhood in the city's east end and pushing ahead with a major redevelopment scheme that will demolish Chinatown, one of the city's most colorful ethnic quarters.

Heritage Canada could turn out to be one of the most important things that has ever happened to the cause of cultural preservation in this country. Established in 1973 with the aid of a $12 million federal grant, it could, given proper leadership and encouragement, eventually evolve into a Canadian version of Britain's National Trust.

But while some federal planners see Heritage Canada as the hope of the future for preserving the best of our cultural wealth, others are pushing development projects that will inevitably lead to the destruction of important buildings and viable communities.

An example is Ottawa's vast new office complex, Place Guy Favreau, which will destroy Montreal's Chinatown. The area between Dorchester, Lagauchetière, St. Urbain and Jeanne Mance has been expropriated and will be razed so that construction can begin by 1976. That will mean the demolition of all three of Chinatown's churches and several of its businesses. It will also mean the disruption of an entire community, but the federal government doesn't seem terribly concerned about that.

"The whole area was getting downtrodden anyway," said a spokesman for the Department of Public Works, explaining why the project is going up in Chinatown.

Place Guy Favreau will be built in several phases, with the first scheduled for completion by 1978. When finished, it will provide one million square feet of office space for about 45,000 workers, plus an assortment of stores, restaurants, cinemas and parking garages.

"We want to keep the area lively, prevent it from becoming a government ghetto when the offices close at 4.30," said the public works official. Costs for the complex have not been revealed because they are under review, he added. So are designs for the buildings.

The government considered several other sites for the complex, including the Grey Nuns Convent on Dorchester Blvd. But the final location was selected for a number of reasons according to Public Works Minister President C.M. Drury.

First, it will help to shift the focus of development in Montreal to the east instead of the north and west. In this way, it will fit into Mayor Drapeau's plans for injecting new life and more money into the area.

Second, the site is the right size, compared with other possible development locations.

"We had to have a large space," says Drury, "to accommodate all the federal workers in Montreal. Right now, they are scattered

Chinatown... to be replaced by federal government offices

all over the city and we hope to improve the government's efficiency by consolidating them."

There is always the possibility the government will need more office space in the future, he adds. If so, it might consider converting the Grey Nuns Convent or some similar building into offices.

For the moment, however, federal authorities continue to favor the large-scale demolition and construction routine.

Maison de Radio-Canada, new headquarters for the CBC on Dorchester Blvd. East, is an example of what going that route entails. It is a prime instance of how development should not take place.

Just why the building was erected on that particular site is still unclear. The federal government was not directly involved in the site selection, although Ottawa had to approve the location before the crown corporation could begin construction.

In October, 1958, the CBC told the City of Montreal that it was anxious to find a 17-acre site in the center of the city where it could consolidate offices and studios into one building. The city offered an area bounded by Dorchester, Bleury, Clark and Vitre, but the CBC turned it down, mainly because the building would have had to occupy both sides of Dorchester.

In May, 1960, the corporation decided it preferred a site further east, bounded by Dorchester, Wolfe, Craig and Papineau. Why and by whom the site was suggested is murky. CBC officials say they don't know. The reluctance to claim responsibility for the choice of the site is perhaps not surprising in view of the fact that its selection eventually brought about the displacement of thousands of families who had been living in the area.

In any event, the CBC's board of directors approved purchase of the site on December 31, 1961, one day after the City of Montreal approved expropriation plans. A few months later, the federal government voted $2,150,000 for the purchase and clearing of the land.

Then followed a saga of nearly 10 years of delays, indecision and disputes. In 1965, after 1,250 homes had been demolished and an entire neighborhood wiped out, the CBC suspended work on the project while it debated its future in the light of the findings of the Fowler Royal Commission on Broadcasting. As a direct result of the Commission's report, the federal government asked the CBC to change its plans for the building. The CBC refused. The issue seesawed back and forth for months until Ottawa finally gave a new go-ahead and excavation was begun in October, 1966.

That work had been completed and the foundation supports put into place when, in the summer of 1967, the City of Montreal decided that zoning by-laws in the area would have to be amended before construction could continue. That caused yet another delay. It was almost another year before the CBC got federal permission to call for tenders so that actual construction could begin.

The building wound up costing $73 million, $13 million over the original budget.

Ever since it was opened it has been criticized both for its design and its location.

Its design brought the one-word comment "appalling" from Joe Baker, McGill architecture professor and head of the school's Community Design Workshop. Other architects have criticized its vast, inhuman scale. Entering Maison de Radio-Canada, one pointed out, is rather like being swallowed up in a huge, dark canyon.

Before the CBC came on the scene, the area where the building now stands was a working-class community—not elegant by any means but an area where low-rental housing was available close to the city core. After expropriation and demolition, the site turned into a bleak desert which sat idle for years, a scar on the face of the city. Now it has become a giant parking lot with a high-rise tower in the middle.

"We keep on doing the same thing," says architect and town planner Jean-Claude LaHaye. "We keep on putting up these huge office buildings, tiny islands in a sea of cars. The CBC headquarters should have been in the center of town, where the action is."

Maison de Radio-Canada consolidated facilities and personnel from more than twenty locations all over the city in a 23-storey hexagonal tower, with two smaller buildings at its base. Employees tend to be pleased with the technical facilities in the new building, which are among the most modern in the world. But they are unhappy about the building's location and the impersonal surroundings.

The French and English television newsrooms, for example, are stuck in the basement of the building and a temperamental ventilation system often makes breathing and thinking difficult after a few hours. Because of the building's size, reporters have to run an endurance course to deliver film and tapes to studios and editing and cutting rooms.

According to the planners, the CBC's location was chosen to encourage new life and development in the east end of the city —the same rationale that is now being applied to the construction of Place Guy Favreau on top of Chinatown. But all the evidence indicates that the CBC development has had no such impact.

What has actually happened is the classic story of most large development projects in areas that authorities like to brand as "run-down."

An entire neighborhood has been wiped out, and thousands of people displaced. Increased traffic congestion has been created by the approximately 3,000 employees going to and from work. Noises are being made about encouraging high-rise apartment development in the area, to provide housing for CBC employees. As that happens, the area and its residents will become more affluent, causing evaluations and taxes to rise. That will lead inevitably to the demolition of more and more low-cost housing, with the less affluent continuing to be squeezed out and no alternative accommodation for them provided.

The federal government shows little concern about this whole process. "Maintaining neighborhoods is not the government's responsibility," says Mr. Drury. "It is too bad they are eliminated but it is up to individuals to preserve them."

Drury's attitude is that asking the federal government to preserve neighborhoods or protect historic buildings is asking taxpayers to pay for things that are not of direct benefit to them. Taxpayers, in fact, do that all the time, but that point seems to escape the minister in this case.

Conservationists often wonder why the federal government can find huge sums of money to eliminate thousands of private homes in the interest of new development projects but cannot see its way clear to using its huge financial resources and expropriation powers for preservation.

One reason may be the buck-passing mentality in Ottawa. No one can seem to agree on just whose responsibility it is to protect Canadian heritage.

Few Canadian cities have the power to protect historic sites and buildings. The provincial government has such power in the Cultural Property Act. But it pleads poverty and passes the buck to Ottawa, saying that's where the money is. The federal government, however, tends to disclaim responsibility and to pass the buck back to private citizens.

"Finding new uses for old buildings is the best way to preserve them," says Drury. But there is little encouragement from Ottawa for people to do that. There is no method of financial compensation, no tax exemptions, no federal arrangements or federal-provincial agreements for helping private individuals to carry out historic restorations. Nor is the government setting an active example or it would have made a stronger effort to obtain the Grey Nuns Convent and convert it to office space.

But here the split personality enters again. While help is not available for individuals interested in restoration, the Department of Regional Economic Expansion is carrying out several projects in Quebec under the guise of encouraging tourism that are really directed at preserving cultural heritage. The restoration of Place Royale in Quebec City is the best example.

Then there is Heritage Canada, which could be a fascinating experiment.

The organization's executive director is Robert A.J. Phillips, a career civil servant who has been head of Information Canada, an assistant secretary to the cabinet, director of northern administration in the Department of Indian Affairs and Northern Development and a long-time officer in the External Affairs Department. A cross-stitched sampler on his office wall seems to sum up the philosophy he brings to the Heritage Canada job: "Ya gotta expect losses."

The reason for the losses is fundamental—Heritage Canada has very little money. Without funds, the organization is powerless to prevent the destruction of historic buildings and sites by intervening to purchase them. Phillips estimates it may be several years before Heritage Canada is in a position to play that kind of active role in conservation work in this country.

In the meantime, the organization is going to keep a low profile—"exerting a quiet backroom influence," is the way Phillips puts it.

First priority will be to push for better preservation laws. Canada's are the "weakest in the world," Phillips says, adding: "Even Australia and Barbados are more alive with preservation than this country."

Within Canada, few of the provinces have good laws to protect history and culture. Quebec's Cultural Property Act is the best on paper, Phillips feels, but it is not being fully used. The Ontario government created a Heritage Foundation six years ago and will soon introduce new cultural protection legislation. Alberta recently passed a preservation law. Most other provinces rely on local volunteer groups.

Heritage Canada is producing a "brown paper" based on research in the provinces and the U.S. which can serve as a guide for future laws.

Phillips feels good preservation laws must be based on three pillars: a comprehensive list of what needs to be preserved, authority to preserve buildings, and compensation for their owners, who lose marketability once a property is protected.

The comprehensive list is almost complete. It is being compiled by the Canadian Inventory of Historic Buildings, part of the National Historic Sites Service in the Parks Department. The inventory was begun in 1970 and to date has computerized data on more than 100,000 buildings all across the country.

Heritage Canada is completely independent of the federal government. It was incorporated on April 2, 1973, and given a $12 million grant to get started. The annual budget comes from interest on the grant, plus private donations, which does not add up to a lot of money. It has its headquarters on the second and third floors of the 1885 Grant House on Ottawa's busy Elgin St. There is a staff of twelve to take care of research and administration work and to look after the membership list which now numbers about 20,000.

When Heritage Canada first began, it asked all the various small historic and preservationist groups across the country for their lists of members. The organizations were invited to join Heritage Canada, and their members were automatically enrolled. Several hundred other individuals were asked to join, but there has been no massive membership campaign.

"We felt we had to have something to offer them first," Phillips explains.

One of the major problems in Canada, Phillips feels, is that few people have yet realized the potential value in preservation. Canadians only started discovering their history in 1967 and while they would like to see it preserved, they're worried about who is going to pay for it.

The question should not be: Can we afford to conserve? he says. It should be: Can we afford not to?

The staff of Heritage Canada has been researching the state of historic conservation across the country, trying to determine what kind of a structure the organization should have. Phillips himself spent a month travelling in the U.S., France and Britain after his appointment, finding out what other countries are doing.

He discovered the U.S. has a national trust formed in 1947 which owns about eleven properties, mostly museum houses. The U.S. National Parks Service owns or operates several dozen more buildings, either on its own or in cooperation with other groups. Many are the birthplaces or homes of former presidents, or death-places, like the house where Abraham Lincoln died.

The National Trust for England, Wales and Northern Ireland, founded in 1895, is the largest private landowner in Britain and has more than 350,000 members. It owns and protects about 420,000 acres of land, several hundred historic homes and large stretches of coastline. The majority of its historic buildings were bequeathed or given in trust.

The National Trust for Scotland was formed in 1931. It owns about 80,000 acres of property and has 50,000 members. "That's nearly 1 percent of the population," notes Phillips, "a really extraordinary figure."

Heritage Canada will be the Canadian version of a national trust, but it will be different from the others.

"We're going to do something to suit the facts of life here," says Phillips. "Families aren't as generous about donating homes as they are in Great Britain and elsewhere. And our tax structure really doesn't make it beneficial for them to do so."

There are other difficulties. No other organization of this kind is faced with such vast geography, such weak laws and such a proliferation of unrelated small groups.

The first steps, therefore, have to be tentative.

At this stage the organization will accept cash donations, gifts or bequests and will foot the maintenance bill for old buildings. Operating homes or other buildings as museums is beyond its means, however. Until enough funds are accumulated to start purchasing buildings and land, there is not much Heritage Canada can do to protect those sites it might one day wish to buy.

For the time being, Heritage Canada can only be an advisory body, providing research and contact for local groups and helping to suggest new uses for older buildings. Phillips says his organization can also provide a "moral" influence, making Canadians aware of the importance of preserving their heritage.

"Our main objective is to save not the past but the future," he says.

At the moment, the body with the main responsibility for maintaining Canada's heritage is the 13-member National Historic Sites and Monuments Board. It is part of the Parks Department and acts as an advisory body to the Minister of Indian Affairs and Northern Development.

The Board, created in 1919, is headed by Peter H. Bennett, former director of the Stratford Festival. Most of its members are history professors, but there is one architect. None is from Montreal.

The Board can classify buildings in three ways. All its decisions must be approved by the minister.

Buildings judged to be of great national importance are acquired and maintained by the government. Most are homes of former prime ministers or historical figures, and there are only six in the entire country. The home of Sir George-Etienne Cartier, one of the Fathers of Confederation, is the only building so maintained in Montreal. The house on Notre Dame St. East was bought in 1973 and is in the process of being renovated.

The Board has also acquired the Laurier home in St. Lin des Laurentides, Quebec; Sir John A. Macdonald's home in Kingston; Mackenzie King's Woodside in Kitchener; Homestead, the Sas-

165

katchewan residence of the first western agriculture minister; and Pope house in Charlottetown.

An additional 30-odd buildings and sites are maintained through cooperative agreements with non-profit organizations. The federal government pays up to 50 percent of the purchase cost. The only Montreal site in this category is the Railway Transportation Museum at Delson, on the South Shore.

Since its inception, the Board has also placed 647 plaques on buildings found to be of historic or architectural importance. However, no compensation is available for owners and no protection of the building is involved. In theory, a plaque can be erected one day and the building demolished the next.

Nor is there any protection for the nearly 100,000 buildings which have been catalogued in the computerized Canadian Inventory of Historic Buildings. Approximately 4,000 of these are in Montreal.

The federal government regards the inventory as phase one. Phase two will include detailed surveys of interiors. Eventually, the most outstanding and historically important will be classified and given protection. Unfortunately, there is no guarantee they will still be standing by then.

Many more historic buildings are going to fall unless the federal government abandons its low profile approach and miserly ways and comes to the conclusion that a country's roots and evolution are just as important as the Gross National Product. Until then, both the history of Montreal and the Canadian identity will suffer.

Chapter Fourteen
The Drapeau Style

Running a city is rather like keeping house. Some people run their homes efficiently and neatly, with meticulous attention to detail. Others are sloppy about it. They sweep dust under the rug and buy lots of new furniture to hide the disorder.

A city is just a bigger home. And there appears to have been a lot of dust swept under the rug at Montreal's City Hall and a lot of new furniture, like the 1976 Olympics, bought to distract attention from the mess.

For the past several years, Montreal has been holding "open house" for everyone who wanted to drop in, including building developers of all sizes and descriptions. But now the public is starting to realize that not all the guests should be welcomed quite so eagerly, and there are signs the politicians at City Hall are starting to pull in the welcome mat and turning their attention to cleaning up the mess inside.

When city council approved by-law 3411 in January, 1974, and a few months later took steps to limit development in the Crescent St. area, it marked the first move by the Drapeau administration to place some controls on the current building boom. Until then, City

Hall had adopted a hands-off policy towards the developers who were changing the face of the downtown area.

By-law 3411 was the city's first genuine attempt to impose tougher standards. The law places controls on the size of residential towers in the downtown area by limiting the amount of floor space allowed, in proportion to the size of the lot. It contains several loopholes and permits are still being issued for the kind of building the by-law was supposed to have prohibited. But, while far from ideal, the by-law was welcomed by environmental groups as a first step towards firmer controls.

The city still has a long way to go, however, if the current development boom is to be brought under control.

The amount of demolition and new construction going on sometimes gives Montrealers the impression that a handful of developers are playing a giant Monopoly game with the city. So far, though, complaints have been met with a few sympathetic statements, two positive acts by city council and more than a little resistance.

The heart of the problem lies within City Hall. Until the stunning election result of November 10, 1974, Montreal's city government was essentially a modern parallel to Versailles in the days of Louis XIV—one-man dictatorial rule prevailed. All the city councillors belonged to one party — the Mayor's Civic Party —leaving little room for disagreement with his policies.

Mayor Drapeau not only had the municipal politicians sewn up. He also kept his civil servants on a very short leash. City employees are required to take a secrecy oath and are forbidden to make public statements or to speak to the press. Not all city employees obey these instructions, but those who don't run the risk of a sharp reprimand from the Mayor's office.

This is particularly hard on members of Montreal's Housing and Planning Department. Many of them disagree with the way development is going in Montreal and would like to speak out publicly against it. But they do not have the freedom to do so, and it takes a very brave public servant to risk incurring the wrath of Mayor Drapeau. Nor are the city planners given the authority they need to control zoning and provide the direction that planning and new construction should have in Canada's largest city.

The rule within the city government up until November 10, 1974, was that whatever Mayor Drapeau wanted, Mayor Drapeau got. He wanted to use Viau Park, one of the largest expanses of green space in the east end, for the Olympic Village in 1976. Housing and Planning Director Guy Legault found the idea appalling and courageously spoke out in public against the plan. His views were taken up by provincial Environment Minister, Dr. Victor Goldbloom, who also voiced his objections. A master plan drawn up by the Montreal Urban Community recommended the park be preserved as badly-needed open space.

Drapeau simply ignored the criticism. He made it brutally clear to Legault that he should keep quiet about the subject and humiliated Goldbloom by publicly unmasking him as a paper tiger without a shred of power to intervene despite his cabinet position. The plan was pushed through and the mayor performed all sorts of intellectual gymnastics trying to demonstrate to Montrealers that more green space would actually be created by cutting up one of the city's few public golf courses and building pyramid-shaped apartment complexes on it.

"There is no real democracy here," said Michel Chevalier, a professor of urban planning at the University of Montreal and a veteran of citizen politics. "Things used to be done with payoffs in city government. Now they are done behind closed doors and the attitude is: 'We know best.'"

Naturally, the mayor doesn't buy that.

"If things happen in this city, it is because I capture the real needs and wishes of the people at large. I try to read their minds and do what is best for them, what they want me to do. That is the way it works in a democracy," he says.

Mayor Drapeau has been credited with putting Montreal on the map, cleaning up its crime, attracting billions of investment dollars. With Drapeau in office, the city has had a renaissance: now there are clean streets, major league baseball, a rejuvenated Old Montreal, impressive new developments, a Metro system and Man and His World.

But Chevalier, who was on the Montreal Citizens Committee which originated Expo, says the mayor takes too much credit.

"Montreal didn't do Expo, Canada did," he says. "The mayor can see ideas but he has no sense, no discrimination."

What Drapeau did enjoy prior to November 10 was power — lots of it.. A story that used to circulate within the city government had two business executives arriving for a meeting with the mayor. They are met by Duc, the mayor's large and aggressive dog, which accompanies him everywhere.

Drapeau sternly commands the beast to lie down and Duc does so, meekly. One executive turns to the other and says: "See, training him to be a city councillor."

Signs of rebellion started to appear in the ranks of the Civic Party even before the November vote, however, indicating that the Drapeau autocracy was coming to an end. The results of the balloting confirmed that—the startling upsurge of the strange coalition known as the Montreal Citizens Movement has ensured that whatever the Mayor does in the future will have to be explained and accounted for.

The new city council has a number of serious problems to deal with. One of the biggest is that the city has no control over demolition. That makes the task of anyone concerned with the preservation of older, low-rise buildings extremely difficult.

Montreal cannot legally refuse to issue a demolition permit to anyone who files an application and pays a $5 fee. This is in sharp contrast with Toronto, New York, Boston and several other North American cities where a building owner must show reason for demolition before a permit is granted.

A Toronto by-law introduced in July, 1974, proposed to make it an illegal act to demolish any residential building without council permission or an appeal to the Ontario Municipal Board. In New York, all applications for demolition permits are made public and opponents have a chance to air their views at open judicial hearings.

But in Montreal, "anyone who wants to demolish a building can do so, no questions asked," according to a Permits Department spokesman.

"You could ask for a permit on the Sun Life Building even though you don't own it, and probably get one."

Demolition permits are transferable. When a building is sold, the permit goes with it. Some owners apply for demolition permits as regularly as they pay their water tax.

"They may have no intention of demolishing, but they get a permit just in case they change their minds," said a city employee. "And for some reason, buildings are more valuable and easier to sell with a demolition permit on the property," he added.

Even though permits are easy to obtain, some owners don't bother. The manager of one of the city's busiest demolition companies says he has torn down "dozens" of buildings on which no permit was ever issued. Demolishing without a permit is considered a violation of zoning regulations. Anyone caught doing so is subject to a fine equal to the permit's cost: $5. He can also be hauled into municipal court but, because of the legal backlog, he usually has plenty of time to complete the demolition before that happens.

In order to obtain the power to refuse demolition permits, the City of Montreal would have to obtain an amendment to its charter, something city officials have been promising to do for some time. So far, no formal application has been made to Quebec City.

City Hall has a list of approximately 600 buildings it considers worth saving, but which it will not make public. It was drawn up by the Planning Department, and each request for a demolition permit is checked against it. Buildings which have been classified by the Quebec Department of Cultural Affairs cannot be demolished without permission from the minister and in such cases—and such cases alone—the city can refuse to issue a permit. But it has no authority to withhold permits on any other buildings, whether they are included on the inventory of historic structures or not. In fact, demolition permits have been issued for buildings supposedly on the city's "protected" list.

The city's inventory was drawn up as a response to the public outcry over the demolition of the Van Horne house. However, without city control over demolition permits it is ineffective, especially when people aren't even told which buildings are on it.

Public knowledge of zoning changes is similarly inhibited. At present, zoning by-laws in the City of Montreal are changed at the instigation of "interested parties" and approved after two meetings of council.

Legal notices are published in the papers, but unless people are extremely interested and take the trouble to search them out, such notices pass unobserved. Some municipalities hold referendums whenever changes in zoning laws are proposed, but the City of Montreal does not. The public thus has no recourse to stop such changes from going through.

In practice, what usually happens is that a developer who wants to erect a high-rise in a low-rise zoned area asks the city to change the regulations for the site he is interested in. Because a high-rise office building means more in tax revenue than a two-storey private house, the change is usually made without fuss or fanfare.

One such change in a district usually brings a flood of applications for more in its wake. Because of the city's tax structure, the whole area eventually ends up rezoned.

Zoning is a device for regulating the use of land and buildings. But as practiced by the City of Montreal, zoning discriminates against low-rise buildings and is open to wide-scale abuses.

It works this way: taxes are levied on the potential revenue a piece of property will generate. When a piece of land is rezoned from residential to commercial or from low-rise to high-rise, its income potential is increased.

A 15-storey building contains much more rentable space than a three-storey one, so its income potential is greater. On that basis, the land on which the building stands becomes more valuable and its evaluation rises.

A piece of property next to a high-rise building also increases in value, but the building on the site does not. Eventually, however, the owner of a private house in the midst of high-rise developments may find himself unable to pay taxes on his increasingly valuable property and sells out—for yet another high-rise building.

A master plan might reduce some of this pressure, but the municipal government is resistant to the concept, even though Montreal is required by law to have a master plan. Article 11 of by-law 4369, passed in January, 1972, states: "The Housing and City Planning Department is responsible for keeping a general plan or master plan up to date."

But no plan is kept up to date for the simple reason that none exists.

The city does a lot of planning, but only on the basis of individual projects. There is no general plan for the City of Montreal, only zoning regulations and by-laws. Of these, the closest thing to a master plan is the mountainside by-law, which regulates the height of buildings on the side of Mount Royal. But even this regulation is not strictly enforced, as evidenced by the number of high-rises encroaching on the mountain's slopes.

Montreal avoided many of the mistakes made by other North American cities because it developed more slowly. But when it did start developing, everything seemed to happen at once.

"There wasn't time to make a master plan," says Aimé Desautels, Montreal Urban Community Planning Director and former director of the City Planning Deparment. "The city has been zoning for almost a century but the Planning Department wasn't created until 1941. Then it was kept busy with the housing boom during and after World War II."

Now, however, there is a strong feeling the time has come to enforce the by-law and to proceed with the drawing up of a master plan for the city.

"There is an urgent need to decide where growth is going to take place," says planner Jean-Claude LaHaye.

The Montreal master plan should designate those areas of the city most in need of development. A recent survey showed that 40 percent of the downtown area consists of vacant lots, available for development. Yet this available space is being ignored in favor of a few, concentrated areas.

"Development brings profit to a small number of people," says LaHaye. "There are a lot of vacant lots because private enterprise is holding them with hopes of making huge profits."

LaHaye advocates a system of controlling profits and land values, which was one of the proposals in the master plan he prepared for the province. His scheme calls for the public retention of titles to all land and the granting of long-term leases. On expiration of the leases, the land reverts back to the public.

Private enterprise can hardly be expected to rush enthusiastically to support such a radical scheme. But at least one Montreal project is currently being built on the basis of this principle. This is Complexe Desjardins, which is going up near Place des Arts on land leased from the city for 60 years. LaHaye, incidentally, is the architect.

Quebec, says LaHaye, should follow British Columbia's lead and adopt a public land ownership policy. At the moment, there are no controls on land use and development in the province. Montreal is at the same stage reached by other North American cities more than a decade ago.

If Montreal doesn't move to enforce some degree of public control on land development, it will end up in deep trouble.

Manhattan master planner Richard Weinstein says Montreal has not yet begun to destroy itself "but if it continues the way it is going for ten years, it will be disastrous. It would be a pity if Montreal doesn't learn from other cities that have choked themselves to death."

Urban planner Vincent Ponte counters criticism that Montreal is growing too quickly with an example from history.

"We admire London now, but at one time Queen Elizabeth I thought it was growing too fast," he says. "She declared a moratorium on all construction. But London grew despite the Queen."

He also cites the broad avenues and vistas of Paris, created under Napoleon III by Baron Haussmann by "rooting people out of their homes, with no compensation."

"All the great cities of the world were created by kings and emperors—who had taste," he says.

Planning for the future is imperative," says Ponte, but "you just can't stop everything. You have to let development continue. There are too many investments, too much money at stake."

So far, the Drapeau administration has shown little interest in adopting any master planning concept for the city at all. This has led to accusations that the mayor favors big business over the retention of neighborhood life, a suggestion he scoffs at.

"It isn't true," he says. "There are still places where people dance in the streets during the summer. Of course there are always some areas that become dilapidated, whose use changes, like Milton-Park. Then the people have to move."

The city's urban renewal policy in such cases has traditionally followed the bulldoze and rebuild approach. Large sections of the city still bear the scars of various renewal experiments—Little Burgundy is a prime example.

Little Burgundy was once a fashionable section of the city. Now, however, much of its turn-of-the-century architecture has been demolished, or is in a state of disrepair. Whole blocks have been bulldozed and then left vacant. The area is like a desert, interspersed with oases of new, anonymous low-income housing units. Commerce and social services are at a minimum.

The city's attitude towards Little Burgundy has been paternalistic. Residents had little say in the plans and projects which ultimately determine how they are to live. Now, however, the city says it has learned from past mistakes and is embarking on a different tack. With Central Mortgage and Housing Corporation, it has instituted something called Neighborhood Improvement Programs. The theory is to help residents to renovate older, existing buildings rather than tearing them down. In principle, it seems like a fine idea. In practice, it works rather differently.

Only one such project has been completed so far in Little Burgundy. It was done in cooperation with a private developer and wound up costing much more than anticipated. Residents, who believed they would have jobs helping to renovate their own greystone townhouses, were shunted aside in favor of outsiders. When the project was completed, rents were raised beyond their means. Original tenants, some of whom had lived in their house for 20 years, had to move out and the restored buildings were snatched up by families from higher income groups. Long-time residents of Little Burgundy were deprived of their homes and their neighborhood by a project which was supposed to have helped them.

While the City of Montreal doesn't discourage private renovation of older buildings, it doesn't actually encourage it either. Two kinds of subsidies are available for Montrealers who want to rejuvenate older buildings. One is for work within the confines of Old Montreal; the other is for renovation of older residential buildings anywhere in the city. Neither program is well-publicized and recipients of both types of grants complain that the city is slow to fork over the money but quick to hike the tax evaluation of the property once the work has been completed.

The city's program of residential renovation began in 1969. In the years up to 1974, $3 million was spent and 2,498 homes were renovated. Budget for the program in fiscal 1974 was $2 million. The city will pay 25 percent of the cost of renovation as long as a homeowner spends $2,000. It will also pay 50 percent of the assessed valuation of an old building if the owner wants to demolish it and can prove that the structure does not conform to the municipal housing code.

Mayor Drapeau lauds the program as the only one of its kind on the continent, but there has been no great effort to spread the word about or to encourage people to renovate their homes. So far, the city has shown no sign of extending such aid to private developers, to discourage demolition of older buildings. And businessmen who take on the tedious task of renovation receive no compensation from City Hall either.

Hotelier André Villeneuve knows from experience that the city discourages people from finding new uses for old buildings.

In 1958, Villeneuve bought the first of four vintage townhouses on Sherbrooke St. Two more were acquired in 1970 and the last one in 1972. All have been renovated and turned into the Chateau Versailles Hotel.

Walls were taken out to join the buildings as one unit and turn-of-the-century details restored. With artistic help from his wife, Marie-Louise, and meticulous attention to detail, Villeneuve has created the equivalent of the perfect little "pension" much sought after by tourists in Paris.

"But it hasn't been easy. City by-laws intended to prevent Sherbrooke St. from degenerating are now holding it back severely by limiting the use of older buildings," says Villeneuve.

"The best uses for such buildings are as museums, clubs and small hotels," he says. "I understand why there are strict laws about using these old buildings as hotels. If they were too lenient anyone could rent a place for $500, call it a hotel and start a bordello."

But he feels there are too many laws and regulations and they are applied without concern for the individual.

There is, for example, a city regulation which states that a hotel must contain 50,000 square feet of space to qualify for a permit. Anything smaller is a rooming house. With only 38,000 square feet, Chateau Versailles is classed as a rooming house, although it has a dining room and functions as a hotel. The ruling puts Villeneuve at a disadvantage with others in the hotel business. The city should consider each case on its merits, he feels.

Villeneuve's own history is a litany of red tape.

Between 1970 and the purchase of his last house, the city passed a by-law prohibiting additional rooming houses on Sherbrooke St., but Villeneuve was not informed. It took three months of applications, meetings, letters and red tape to get the by-law changed.

Now his only problem is the unusable room. It's in the bottom of the fourth house and is unused because a city by-law stipulates he must have a garage. Inaccessible to cars, it is impossible to use the room as a garage. But it can't be converted into a guest room because of the by-law, so it stays empty, and unproductive.

Villeneuve paid $75,000 for his first house and spent about the same amount restoring it. The last house, virtually identical, cost $300,000 in 1972. The hotel owner estimates he has spent more than $750,000 since starting business, most of it on restoration. He received no financial help from the city and there are no concessions on his annual taxes, which average between $20,000 and $25,000. He says he doesn't want a handout, but he feels the city could do more to stimulate renovation.

Hopes for preserving the city's character hinge on making it economically feasible to do so. The municipal government could encourage individuals and the business sector by increasing the number and the amount of grants it now gives and by granting tax incentives to those who recycle rather than redevelop.

But simply compensating property owners isn't enough. Development must also be controlled through the formulation of a master plan.

The nearest thing to a master plan for the city is a lavish document drawn up for the Montreal Urban Community. But it will never become law because the MUC does not have the authority to legislate in this area. The only function of the plan is as a sort of "moral obligation," providing guidelines for municipalities.

The MUC has no power to curtail or direct development. It can only make recommendations. Legislation has been presented to the Quebec National Assembly which would allow planning to be carried out on three levels: regional, urban community and municipal. Plans at each level will have to conform to those of the others.

"But it is going backwards," says Desautels. "It should have started at the regional level and gone down."

The MUC plan calls for curbing automobile traffic, controlling development and preserving open spaces. It has been criticized for not going far enough, but Desautels says if municipalities adopt only half the proposals "they will have done more towards planning than since Mount Royal was acquired in the early 1900's."

Master planning is a hotly-debated item among governments, planners, developers and citizens. Developers fear anything that smacks of control over their right to build what they like, where they like. Planners fear the possibility of overplanning, which results in a rigid, unworkable structure.

But compromises can be found. The key to master planning lies in the formation of flexible guidelines.

Montreal has the beginnings of a master plan in its mass transit system and in projections for expanding the sheltered city. Additions to it could include:

1. Provisions for preserving historic landmarks.
2. Public ownership of land.
3. Controls on construction.
4. Guidelines for where and how development may take place.
5. Transfer of air rights, as an aid to zoning.
6. A policiy of encouraging development in areas that need it.
7. Aesthetic standards.
8. Increased mass transportation and discouragement of private automobiles.
9. Designation of parkland and green spaces to be preserved or created before they are threatened with development.
10. Emphasis on housing, to prevent street crime and a "dead" city core at night, and to ensure, what urban expert Jane Jacobs calls self-policing action of people who live in the downtown.

One of the most important aspects of master planning is that the public be allowed to participate in it, to approve plans, to protest in open judicial hearings and to have a voice in shaping the environment.

Public participation is already working successfully in at least one Canadian city. Ottawa was the first North American city to institute neighborhood studies, a program involving residents working with planners and developers to determine what new development and alternate transportation routes are needed in their area. These local groups have the right to present alternative development proposals if they disagree with projects prepared by city planners. But final authority rests with Ottawa's Board of Control.

No such experiments have yet been tried in Montreal. But the city is going to have to start thinking seriously about involving the citizens more in the planning for the future. There are numerous problems that need to be solved: housing, traffic, pollution, diminishing resources, inflation, and higher land values. Montrealers are just beginning to realize the potential of their own resources to solve these problems, as is shown by the new wave of citizens' groups and the political alliances seeking urban democracy.

"We are moving towards a new human institution," says architect Michel Lincourt, co-founder of General Urban Systems, a non-profit urban affairs research corporation. "There is an urge to control the environment but our problems can only be solved by making plans visible to the public."

Lincourt predicts that Montreal will one day be a city-state in a whole system of city-states united by world government. He believes Mayor Drapeau understands this concept "in his own way."

"His personal dream of grandeur is linked to it," Lincourt says.

But the city-state is a long way off. At the moment the urgent need is for City Hall to shake itself and start planning for the immediate future needs of Montreal.

Chapter Fifteen

The Turning Tide

Slowly but surely, the tide of citizen action is turning in Montreal.

Ten years ago, no one would have considered protesting the changes taking place in the aspect of the city. Development was welcomed with open arms and blank cheques.

The opening of Place Ville Marie in 1962 started a renaissance in the downtown core which saw four million square feet of office space constructed and $7 million added to the city's tax revenues in just a few years. The building of the Metro and the furious activity which preceded Expo 67 continued the pattern, creating a city that seemed supercharged with energy. Planner Anshel Melamed describes the atmosphere during that period as "like a carnival."

But the carnival is over. The bright lights are dimming and the music is turning sour. The reaction has set in.

Uncontrolled development threatens areas all over the city. The demolition of landmarks and the disruption of neighborhoods are provoking angry outcries.

As a result, citizens' groups have been springing up all over the city. Some are large, some are small, some are more vocal than others but they all share a common purpose: improving

Montreal, making the administration more democratic and thwarting threats to the city's character and beauty.

The grass-roots strength of this trend was clearly demonstrated in the success of the fledgling Montreal Citizens Movement in the civic election of Nov. 10, 1974. Starting late and working from virtually no political base at all, the MCM succeeded in knocking off some of the Drapeau government's leading figures, putting a strong opposition onto city council, and giving the Mayor his toughest fight in years with candidate Jacques Couture, a Jesuit priest turned politician.

The MCM isn't the only force to appear out of the growing trend towards citizen involvement in Montreal. About two dozen community groups have come together in an alliance known as Save Montreal, which in the autumn of 1974 launched a joint appeal with Green Spaces for $250,000 to carry on the fight for preservation in the city.

Save Montreal has been viewed with alarm in some quarters ever since its formation in September, 1973. Its members have been ridiculed and called everything from "green space groupies" to "Van Horne nutniks." They have been dismissed as unrealistic elitists or as welfare recipients with nothing better to do with their time.

One Montreal developer, Joseph Kracauer, summed up this view in an interview published by Canadian Building magazine in May, 1974: "I love this city and I'm trying to help it grow. But it's the protesters that get the publicity. Some of them must be on welfare. They contribute nothing to Montreal. They seem to have all day to think and to get the publicity that makes Montreal's real allies—the builders—look like villains.

"Montreal has the opportunity now to enter a period of unprecedented development. Is it going to take advantage of this opportunity, or be talked into standing still?"

The reality of groups like Save Montreal is much different from this kind of picture. Objectives of these organizations are

The Shaughnessy mansion on Dorchester Boulevard

education, preservation and a better urban environment. There are problems, of course. The diverse member groups of Save Montreal do not agree with one another on the form of action it should be taking or what its priorities should be. Money is scarce, and the budget can best be described as hand-to-mouth. But despite these difficulties, the organization has raised public consciousness and awakened City Hall to the reality of the citizens' movements.

There had been suggestions that Save Montreal would eventually evolve into a political party, but that role has now been fulfilled by the Montreal Citizens Movement, which many Save Montreal members support. The MCM has become symbolic of drastic change in the course of municipal affairs in Montreal —the same kind of change which has already occurred in Toronto and Vancouver.

The Toronto turn-around began in much the same way as the pattern now emerging in Montreal. Citizens groups began springing up all over the city about ten years ago, much as they are appearing now in Montreal. They began as loosely-knit groups of protestors, usually unorganized and ineffectual. But within a few years they had matured into a force powerful enough to force the provincial government to stop the Spadina Expressway and to win control of City Hall. That happened in the 1972 municipal election which brought David Crombie to the mayor's chair and a slate of people-power candidates to a majority on council in an upset that startled the country.

The November civic election indicated that a replay of this scenario may now be underway in Montreal. The city appears to be emerging as the next people-power battleground in Canada.

The reactions from City Hall, even before the November vote, indicated Mayor Drapeau was not unaware of what was happening. But the response of his old city council to the growing demands for action from the Montreal public was sporadic and no action was ever taken on one of the main demands of the preservationists: a total freeze on all demolition in the city and formulation of a publicly approved master plan for development.

This reluctance to react by the Drapeau administration may change drastically as a result of the November election. If nothing else, he now has to face tough questioning at council meetings from MCM members over his party's policies.

Save Montreal, meanwhile, is in the process of completing its organization and trying to attract more support from French-speaking areas of the city where interest in preservation has been only marginal until now.

Save Montreal's membership includes architects, planners, pensioners, students, artists, housewives and people displaced by urban renewal. Some already belonged to citizens' groups when the federation was formed and automatically became members. Others have joined as individuals and begun working with groups that interest them most.

The member organizations include:

Bishop St. Tenants' Association. Originally begun in support of a couple whose Bishop St. greystone was being demolished around them, this organization is waging a vociferous campaign against further development of one of the last low-rise streets in the city core. The street fairs it sponsored during the summer of 1974 drew attention to the cause and raised money in a novel and imaginative way.

Comité des Citoyens de Rivière des Prairies. One of five predominantly French-speaking groups allied to Save Montreal, it was formed in 1972 and now has about 200 members. Its basic purpose is to try to solve the problems of social services, housing and demolition in the north-end community, all of which have been affected by the formation of the Montreal Urban Community. The MUC would like to profit from the abundance of property in the area, so demolition and development are posing major problems.

Comité de Conservation de Montréal. Headed by René Boulay, former vice-president of the Museum of Fine Arts junior associates, the group evolved from an environmental pollution exhibit suggested by the Museum in 1968 but rejected as too touchy. Eventually the project was accepted for display at Man and His World, however. There is no official membership and the Comité is really a loose alliance of businessmen in fields ranging from public relations to tourism. Since 1970, they have been protesting against the use of Viau Park for the 1976 Olympics, without result.

Community Design Workshop. Begun by McGill architecture professor Joe Baker as a practical exercise in design, the workshop has now become part of the school's curriculum. Students work in architectural offices and their projects have included parks, a day-care center and an alternative plan for the Milton-Park area. The program is still going on but suffers from a lack of funds.

Conservation Society of McGill University. In October, 1973, first-year McGill student Lisa Lewis became interested in saving historic buildings on the campus. About fifteen students and several professors joined her and together they produced a dossier on Morrice Hall, built in 1881 and threatened with demolition. McGill is still debating the building's future.

Esplanade Residents Association. Formed in November, 1973, its prime concern is preserving the environment of Esplanade St. and the area bordering Fletcher's Field. Members come from a variety of ethnic and socio-economic backgrounds. Their aim is to change zoning laws before large-scale high-rise development threatens their unique neighborhood.

Faubourg Cherrier. The architecture and ambience of an area bounded by Lafontaine Park, St. Louis Square, Mount Royal Ave. and Viger Square is the particular concern of this east-end preservationist group.

Friends of Windsor Station. Since 1971, this association of 400 Montrealers, headed by architects Peter Lanken and Michael Fish, has been trying to save this landmark building. Their protests appear to have made an impression because the CPR is now reexamining development plans which called for the station's demolition, and a consultant's report has recommended keeping at least part of the structure.

Greene Avenue Village Association. Formed in the summer of 1974, the group opposes further large-scale development such as the Westmount Square complex, designed by Mies van der Rohe and owned by Mondev Corporation. Mondev already has expropriated several small shop owners for expansion and the citizens group fears, others will follow, with an end to the village-like shopping atmosphere.

Green Spaces. Originally formed to protest development on land owned by the Sulpician Order, the 350-member organization headed by Denise Faille has also been concerned with finding an alternative to the use of Viau Park for the Olympics and with increasing the amount of green space in the entire city. With Viau Park included, Montreal has an average of 2.6 acres of green space per 1,000 inhabitants, far below the desirable standard of 10 acres per 1,000.

Griffintown People's Association. In an area which has been zoned for industrial use, a small group of people has been working since 1970 to bring social services to the district. About 187 families live in Griffintown, most of them elderly, and their main problem is housing. The area is rich in history, but it is deteriorating badly.

Haddon Hall Tenants Association. George Seaden, a consulting engineer who lives in Haddon Hall, a stately Sherbrooke St. apartment house, led residents' protests when the building changed hands and demolition seemed imminent. Demolition has now been delayed for at least three years but the group intends to continue doing all it can to preserve the residence.

The 210 apartments in the building form a community of about 900 people, 60 percent to 70 percent of whom participate actively in the organization.

Human Rights for Senior Citizens. Approximately 600 senior citizens have been trying for more than two years to get a better deal from society. They are campaigning for the preservation of older buildings and low-cost housing as well as for lower bus fares and pension rights. The group's leader is 67-year-old John E. Pearson.

Logeantoine. Begun by Community Design Workshop member Bob Stanley, Logeantoine is a cooperative housing project for Lower Westmount. Its aim is to replace houses demolished for the east-west autoroute with renovated buildings.

Lower Westmount Citizens Committee. This ad hoc group originated in 1969 when the autoroute began cutting a swath through the area. It has saved several housing units which it wants to restore in cooperation with Logeantoine. But it has also had losses, buildings that were demolished by the Quebec Transport Department even though they were no longer in the path of a proposed access road.

McGregor Avenue Tenants Association. When tenants of several stately homes, converted to apartments, were faced with eviction in the summer of 1974, they formed a citizens group. They appealed to the Quebec Rental Board and the provincial government. One building was classified by the Ministry of Cultural Affairs, thus prohibiting demolition of the others. All the buildings are owned by an absentee West German landlady. The citizens group is now concerned with preserving the rest of the character of Montreal's once-elegant Embassy Row.

Milton-Park Citizens Committee. This group originated in 1968 when Concordia Estates began planning massive demolition and urban renewal in the Milton-Park area. Chairperson Lucia Kowaluk estimates only 50 people are active now compared to 300 who occupied the construction site a few years ago and who were arrested for their efforts.

Montreal Society of Architecture. With 125 professional and student members, this organization is concerned with changing the philosophy of the profession. It offers advice on buildings and has prepared a guidebook emphasizing Montreal's unique architecture.

Save the Main Research Committee. Begun as an outgrowth of the Save the Main project, the five-member committee headed by Brian McCarthy is gathering data on property owners and evaluations along St. Lawrence Blvd. The aim is to deter property assembly and to prevent the destruction of one of Montreal's most colorful ethnic areas.

Society for the Preservation of Great Places. Begun during the struggle to save the Van Horne mansion, the group now numbers about 300. It waged a campaign to save the Shaughnessy mansion on Dorchester Blvd., which ended with the building's classification by the provincial government.

Somerset-Lincoln Street Tenants Association. Like the Bishop St. and Haddon Hall groups, this organization was formed as a direct response to development which threatened the neighborhood. Residents of a low-rise apartment building banded together when part of the structure was sold for high-rise construction, in an effort to stop the move.

Stanley Street Committee. Members of Alpha Delta Phi fraternity at McGill formed the committee as a public service project. A small research team of twelve members is gathering historical information on the street which they hope to publish.

St. Hubert, Carré St. Louis Association. The unique flavor of quarters such as St. Louis Square is the prime concern of this organization. It has one major victory to its credit: defeat of a proposed high-rise complex which would have destroyed much of the charm of the square.

St. Urbain Community Center. The center is headquarters for about 200 different community projects, ranging from day-care and immigrant aid to housing and renovation.

Student Society, McGill University. Sporadically active, the society joined Save Montreal to aid an ad hoc committee's study of Chinatown. The large number of Chinese students in the school provided impetus.

Terrasse Ontario. Begun in 1972, the group describes itself as an "operation grand menage." Its main interest is the renovation of lower-income housing.

Apart from all these participating groups, another aspect of the Save Montreal movement is the *Centre de référence et d'information sur l'environnement* (CRISE). This is a research group that began as a local initiatives project in January, 1974. When the LIP grant expired, the group continued as an Opportunities for Youth project, collecting and disseminating information on demolition, development and the environment. If and when additional sources of funds are found after the expiration of the OFY grant, the work will be carried on in coordination with Save Montreal.

Save Montreal, despite its handicaps, is the most organized and coherent citizens' action organization to appear to date. But the oldest, formed long before the public ever became aware of the dangers of wholesale demolition and uncontrolled development, is Canadian Heritage of Quebec. Without fanfare or publicity, it has been quietly rescuing old buildings and natural sites.

The people who started it didn't wait for a government task force report on the need for conservation. They didn't wait for government funds either. They saw what had to be done, pooled their resources, and did it.

In 1955, Colin J.G. (Jack) Molson, president of the Canadian Guild of Crafts, learned that one of the oldest houses on the Island of Montreal was threatened. He inquired about saving it and was told there was nothing the City of Montreal or the Municipality of Westmount, where it was located, could do. Convinced that the best way to preserve a building is to own it, Molson persuaded several friends to chip in. Together, they bought and restored the 1689 Hurtubise house at 39 Cote St. Antoine Road, and the Canadian Heritage of Quebec was born.

Within five years, the fledgling organization had acquired two more properties. Both are natural sites on the coast opposite Percé Rock in Gaspé. The rock had been protected by the provincial government. But the nearby shoreline was unprotected and in danger of Coney Island-type development before Molson and his group bought Cap Barré and Cap Mont Joli in the late 1950's. Aside from spectacular natural beauty, the properties have historic value. Jacques Cartier visited Cap Mont Joli on his first voyage in 1534, and Molson and his friends didn't think motels and hot-dog stands were at all appropriate for such an historic piece of coastline.

Titles for the first three properties were held in the names of the original twelve members of the organization. But it soon became apparent there would be a problem when one of them died. As a result, the organization was incorporated in 1960 and its membership opened to the public. It now has about 350 members who donate from $5 up to $1,000 a year. There is a 12-member board of directors, and Molson remains as president.

Titles to all properties are now held in the name of Canadian Heritage of Quebec. At present there are 15 sites. In addition to the three original properties, the organization owns an old Indian camping site, a former British military headquarters, a chapel, a covered bridge and a chunk of beautiful beach on the lower St. Lawrence River. It also owns the "Silver Dollar Saloon" at the corner of Notre Dame St. East and Jacques Cartier Square in Old Montreal. Its floor was once paved with silver dollars but it now leads a more mundane existence as a United Cigar Store. The building was originally bought by Imperial Tobacco and turned over to Heritage.

Another of the organization's properties is the Simon Fraser House in Ste. Anne de Bellevue. Once threatened with destruction to make way for a highway, the building now houses a ground floor tea room run by the Victorian Order of Nurses.

Several other properties in the province are held in private names for Heritage, or under partnership arrangements with owners who agree not to alter or demolish without permission.

The organization's showpiece, however, remains its original acquisition—the Hurtubise house. Before being purchased by Heritage, it had been owned by the same family for over 200 years; now it serves as the organization's headquarters.

The Hurtubise family came to Quebec from France with de Maisonneuve. They were stone masons by profession and built numerous houses in the new settlement, some of which still survive in Old Montreal. There is evidence that they may have built the Sulpician Seminary, next to Notre Dame Cathedral, which displays a style of masonry similar to that of the Hurtubise house.

Molson's group worked long and hard to preserve and restore original parts of the house. But their work has not attracted a great deal of attention because Molson is, by nature, a modest person who does not seek publicity. He is reluctant to discuss the financial aspects of Heritage's work, preferring not to reveal how much has been spent acquiring and restoring various properties. But it is obvious from the way the organization works that none of its money is spent on non-essentials—there are no newsletters, mass meetings or social functions, and administration costs are kept to a minimum. The money and energy are saved for the real job of preservation and restoration.

Like Save Montreal, Molson's group is strictly non-political and has no inclination to change that status. With the emergence of the Montreal Citizens' Movement as a potent force, there will be no need to — presuming the MCM remains intact. That may take a bit of doing. The MCM is a coalition of diverse groups, drawing support from the Parti Québecois, the NPD, the labor movement, the academic community, and a surprisingly large segment of the English-speaking middle class. Its natural tendency will be to splinter into its component parts.

The challenge facing its members until the next municipal elections in 1978 will be to concentrate attention on common reform goals, not on long-standing differences. If the party succeeds in doing that, it could be a genuine challenger for control of council and the mayor's office next time around.

Chapter Sixteen

A Blueprint for Action

"That post-Expo lull may have been the saving of Montreal," wrote *The Gazette's* editorial page editor, Tim Creery, in March, 1974.

"It didn't seem like it at the time. The pace of business growth slackened, and building with it. The extraordinary promise of the late fifties and the sixties seemed to be withering...

"Although an unsettling period, it was also a breathing space, a time for review and reconsideration. People had time to think about what they did not like — as well as what they did —in the earlier period of boom.

"Some old landmarks, old prospects, were missed. The cutting up of neighborhoods for new developments left a feeling of deprivation that spread far beyond the neighborhoods themselves. Some of the new landmarks stuck out like sore thumbs, jarring, unwelcome. Others, as they became tarnished, showed their tinsel quality, like Christmas trees kept beyond Twelfth Night.

"It was during this period too that the cry of the environmentalists for a countryside and city fit to live in was being heard in many lands. In languishing Montreal, not everyone looked upon the bold promoters' blueprints for renewing the old boom with stars in their eyes.

"There was time to be warned by what was happening in a Toronto or a Johannesburg, a Detroit or a Frankfurt. Black, upended crates of buildings. Wall-to-wall pavement. Cold concrete. Opaque windows. Harsh fluorescence by day and night, cold gloom in the shadow of the sky-blockers. Tire-whine on the dizzying throughway. Derelict houses, offices, warehouses. Vacant lots full of junk. The wrecker became the builder, the builder the wrecker.

"There was time to hear the whispers from the storied past, from the Montreal of all our yesterdays—of the explorers, missionaries, fur traders; of windjammers and ocean liners; of revolution, riot and parliament burning; of merchant prince and railway baron; of artist, poet, musician, sculptor, architect; of blizzard and baking summer; of a century, and another century, and another, and part of yet another—whispers saying that what you destroy is gone."

Much of that Montreal has been destroyed and is forever gone. But much of the past that is worth saving remains. Whether it survives depends on the vigilance of the public and the press, on a more concerned attitude in the business community and on the willingness of politicians at all levels to embark on a crash program to strengthen existing laws to protect the environment and to put new structures into place.

None of this will be easy. There must be some degree of encroachment on individual property rights and a recognition that urban land can no longer be regarded as a private commodity in which the public has no stake nor interest. There must be a commitment of more funds, which will have to be obtained either through increased taxation or through a shifting of spending priorities by the various levels of government. Politicians must cede certain powers so that meaningful public bodies with authority to act can be created. These things will not come

Len Sidaway of The Gazette

about easily, and there may be bitter controversy. But if they
do not happen, the cultural heritage of Montreal will vanish in a
cloud of masonry dust.

The aim should not be to stifle development in Montreal.
Every city needs development if it is to grow and to evolve into
a better place in which to live. A city cannot be turned into a
museum; it must remain vibrant if it is to remain alive. But
development must be controlled and directed; it must take
place with reference to the people who must live with it rather
than being dictated strictly by dollar considerations.

As Toronto Mayor David Crombie put it in a speech in the
fall of 1973: "I want to encourage development, but I want it
to be good development.

"Good development is compatible with the area that surrounds it and the current uses of the area. I support that kind of development.

"Good development doesn't strain our public services and overload community systems like parks and open space. I support that kind of development.

"Good development takes the moving of people and the delivery of goods into account and respects the pedestrian environment. I will support that kind of development.

"Good development doesn't replace useful or historical buildings for the sake of one other sterile feat of engineering skill. It forces architects and designers to meet aesthetic challenges rather than reaching into a box of old blueprints and stamping out another skinny steel box. I will support that kind of development."

If Montreal is to achieve the kind of good development described by Mayor Crombie, a number of new programs have to be introduced by the municipal, provincial and federal governments.

On the municipal level, to begin with, immediate action is needed to give the City of Montreal some control over the issuing of demolition permits. At the moment, getting a demolition permit is as easy as obtaining a dog licence; the city passes them out for a fee of $5, subject to a ten-day delay.

Although it is possible to delay the issuing of a permit for a few weeks, the city has no power to refuse an application. This means there is no authority capable of preserving an unclassified building if a request is made to demolish it.

As a priority measure, the City of Montreal should seek, and the provincial government should grant, an amendment to the City Charter giving municipal authorities power to refuse the granting of demolition permits.

The rules of the game need to be adjusted, however, so that a private developer is given ample warning that a particular property of interest to him is liable to be viewed by the city as being of special importance. If municipal authorities are to be given the right to withhold demolition permits, the private sector must in all fairness be given a clear idea of where this power is likely to be exercised.

The City of Montreal, prompted by the Save Montreal organization, has undertaken a detailed inventory of buildings in the regions which are of special architectural or historical interest. Numerous sites have already been placed on the list. But, until now, city officials have refused to make the inventory public.

The city should immediately publish the names of all sites included in the inventory and therefore deemed to be of special importance. The names of any new buildings or sites added at some future date should also be made public.·

It is important that the selection of buildings and sites for the inventory not be left as the sole preserve of politicians and civic officials.

Members of the public should be allowed to submit names of buildings, areas and natural sites for consideration for inclusion in the inventory.

Once a building has been placed on the inventory, it should be provided with some form of protection that is under the control of recognized experts in the field of history and architecture. Granting control over demolition permits to city council will not be enough if the door is left open to abuses.

Montreal already has a body which would be ideally suited to exercise this responsibility—the Viger Commission. Its members are all acknowledged experts in their fields, and they care deeply about the future of the city.

But if the Viger Commission is to play any genuine role in determining the course of development in Montreal, it must be given meaningful powers. New York City's Landmarks Preservation Committee, for instance, has the power to designate structures and districts as historic sites which may not be altered or demolished without permission from the eleven-member body. Some 400 buildings and sites in the city have been so designated, including the Metropolitan Museum, the New York Public Library, the New Dorp Lighthouse on Staten Island and an 85-year-old magnolia tree in Brooklyn. Other American cities, notably New Orleans and Philadephia, have similar committees with substantial powers of action.

A similar body is vital to Montreal if the city's cultural heritage is to be preserved. It should not only be given authority to act, but it should also become the conscience of the city by throwing its deliberations open to the public and releasing all its actions and recommendations to the press.

The Viger Commission should be reconstituted into an organization with authority, modelled on similar public bodies in the United States.

All meetings of the Viger Commission should be open to the public.

All recommendations of the Viger Commission should be released immediately to the press.

The Viger Commission should be given the power to prohibit any demolition or external alteration of buildings and sites on the City of Montreal inventory.

Viger Commission members should have the power to order a temporary halt to any demolition in the city, even if the building is not included on the inventory.

While the Viger Commission should have authority over proposed demolition involving historic buildings, controls are also needed over development projects which may not involve landmark buildings but which may be undesirable for other reasons.

This should be done through the creation of mechanisms to inform the public when important demolition and/or development programs are being planned and to provide for public review of such schemes whenever it is thought desirable.

Developers will contend that such proposals, if implemented, would retard construction and, by causing delays, would add to costs. But if Montrealers are to obtain some say over the direction in which the city is going, these procedures are essential.

The City of Montreal should publish all applications for demolition permits and should allow a suitable delay for objections to be filed before granting such permits.

A permanent review body should be established to examine all applications for demolition not involving historic sites. The body should hold public hearings on applications whenever objections are filed.

All development plans should be deposited with the City Planning Department and made available for public scrutiny at least 60 days before work is permitted to begin.

Where there is objection to development plans, interested parties should be granted a public hearing before the permanent review body, which would have authority to reject the scheme if necessary.

Although a review body is needed to provide a mechanism for public participation in the planning process, the city already has an organization which could be given a more important role to play in the whole process—the Montreal Planning Department.

The Planning Department is staffed with talented, highly-motivated people. But the politicians of the Drapeau administration have frequently ignored their advice and rejected their counsel.

There is little point in taxpayers footing the bill for a skilled, highly-paid body like the Planning Department unless better use is made of it.

The City Charter should be amended so as to give more authority to the Planning Department and to allow publication of its reports and recommendations.

As a priority task, the department should be asked to prepare a report on desirable construction standards to be applied to all future development projects. These should cover safety features, microclimatic effects, the architectural relationship with the surrounding area, open-space ratios and impact on public transit.

The City Planning Department should be asked to prepare a master plan for Montreal, designating areas where development is to be permitted and districts which are to be protected or are subject to rigorous controls. The plan should be made public.

One of the special problems which Montreal will face when it starts to come to grips with its future will be the crisis facing its fine religious buildings. This is a genuine dilemma, complicated by the fact that many of these structures, although architecturally important, do not lend themselves well to alternate uses.

A special committee should be formed to include provincial government representatives, city councillors, church representatives, spokesmen for preservationist groups, representatives of the business community and private citizens. It should examine the problem of religious buildings and prepare a report with specific recommendations for consideration by the various levels of government concerned.

Some sort of system has to be established in the city to provide for the defense of neighborhoods threatened with massive development programs which are not in keeping with the district. Until now, there has been no official recognition of this problem. Various citizens' groups which have been formed in attempts to save a district from destruction have been notably unsuccessful in influencing City Hall to intervene.

Legal recognition should be given to the existence of neighborhoods in Montreal.

Local citizens' groups, where they exist, should be given an opportunity to participate in development plans for their area through a requirement that promoters negotiate with them before depositing final plans with the City Planning Department.

In the past, development programs have often led to the uprooting and forced relocation of hundreds of families. The construction of Maison de Radio-Canada, for instance, was only made possible through the demolition of the homes of over 1,200 families. These people were left on their own to find new accommodation, without any help from government agencies.

A coherent program of relocation assistance should be established by the City of Montreal to help families forced to move by development projects to find new accommodation at comparable rent levels.

Proper use of zoning laws is another key element in controlling the course of development in Montreal. Especially important is the introduction of the concept of discretionary zoning, by which development proposals are measured against standards laid down by the City Planning Department and approved or rejected on the basis of their probable impact on a neighborhood or community.

The city's zoning regulations should be flexible enough to allow for this approach. But they should not be so flexible that they can be amended at the whim of a developer. Major changes in zoning regulations—for instance, rezoning a low-rise area for high-rise buildings—should require extraordinary procedures for approval.

The concept of discretionary zoning should be introduced in Montreal.

Any proposed major change in city zoning laws should be submitted to a referendum before final approval can be granted.

. One of the main problems in preserving old buildings and low-rise development in the city center is the municipal taxation system which promotes bigness and penalizes the little guy. Unless the system is changed to relieve the financial pressure on the mid-town property owner favoring high-rise redevelopment, the chances of retaining many of Montreal's finest buildings are slim.

There should be an end to the practice of levying property taxes on the basis of potential profitability rather than on the basis of existing structures on the site.

The city could further encourage retention and restoration of existing buildings through a meaningful program of grants, loans and subsidies backed up by budgeted, available cash instead of vague promises.

Money should be made available in the City of Montreal budget for providing assistance to owners of buildings, both inside and outside Old Montreal, for restoration work.

The creation of Old Montreal was an excellent idea, and has preserved a fascinating part of the city for posterity. But the area has been left to languish after an early burst of energy and no serious attempt has been made to extend the concept to provide protection for adjacent areas of the city that are now threatened.

The City of Montreal should proceed immediately with plans to improve the appearance of Old Montreal, restore some of its finer buildings and provide the types of essential services that will attract more permanent residents to the area.

The boundaries of Old Montreal should be extended so as to provide protection to St. James St. between St. Lawrence Blvd. and McGill St.

Finally, the city should use the powers it already has more strictly in order to protect the urban environment.

The mountainside by-law, No. 3722, should be strictly enforced so as to prevent any further encroachment by developers on Mount Royal.

The City of Montreal cannot act alone and in a vacuum, however. If Montreal's cultural heritage is to be protected, the provincial government must play a key role as well.

Up to now, Quebec City has abdicated its responsibility in Montreal. The Cultural Property Act, which gives the government the power to protect important buildings and districts, has not been used to anything like its full potential. The Department of Cultural Affairs, starved for funds and attempting to operate on a shoestring budget, has tended to adopt a hands-off approach towards the city and tries to bend over backwards to avoid becoming embroiled in controversial issues.

If the Cultural Property Act is to become a useful instrument in the fight to save the best of what remains in Montreal, this negative posture has to change. The provincial government must revise its priorities to make heritage protection a prime concern and equip the department with the money and personnel it needs to do the job.

Beginning immediately, there should be large annual increments in the budget of the Cultural Affairs Department in order that it may meet its legal responsibilities in the area of heritage preservation.

The Cultural Affairs Department should establish a well-funded grants and incentives program to encourage the restoration of historic buildings and to provide for their continuing maintenance where necessary.

The provincial government should establish an organization in Quebec similar to Heritage Canada and provide it with a substantial endowment.

Amendments should be made to the provincial laws governing income taxes and estate duties to make gifts of property to organizations like Heritage Canada or its Quebec equivalent a more attractive option.

As part of its program for upgrading the importance of cultural preservation in the province, the government must also look at a new and expanded role for the Cultural Property Commission.

At the moment, the Commission might as well not exist. It holds its deliberations in private and contributes nothing to public knowledge on the issues of cultural heritage except once a year when it releases its annual report. Its recommendations to the minister are frequently rejected or, worse, simply ignored. Its members, well-meaning though they may be, are unable to play any active role in the struggle taking place around them. The Commission has no budget and hence no staff to provide technical assistance.

All meetings of the Cultural Property Commission should be opened immediately to press coverage.

All recommendations forwarded to the Minister of Cultural Affairs by the Commission should be released simultaneously to the press.

The provincial government should make provision for a substantial budget for the Cultural Property Commission to enable it to engage staff needed for research and technical work.

The Cultural Property Commission should arrange for the regular publication of learned papers on matters relating to the preservation of Quebec's heritage.

The Cultural Property Commission should sponsor periodic seminars to acquaint the Quebec public better with the issues involved in heritage preservation.

Another area in which the provincial government could act to assist in the preservation of Montreal's historic buildings is the sale of church land to private developers.

Many preservationists feel it is almost immoral for church authorities, who have benefited from generous tax concessions for years, to be selling off fine old buildings and green space to development companies at enormous profit. Some sort of government control on this type of transaction might go a long way towards encouraging reluctant religious officials to think in terms of improving the city's environment rather than making a quick buck.

The provincial government should institute a substantial tax on the proceeds from the sale of church land to private interests for development purposes.

The provincial responsibility for education offers yet another field for potential action by the Quebec government. Montreal's universities — especially McGill and the University of Quebec — have been among the most guilty of the developers in terms of destroying picturesque or valuable buildings for purposes of expansion. Furthermore, many of the new structures that have replaced the lost buildings have been decidedly of third-rate architectural quality, adding little to the central core.

The provincial Department of Education should officially encourage universities to respect the integrity of the surrounding neighborhood when embarking on new capital projects.

Special grants should be established by the provincial government to assist universities in the renovation of older buildings to handle new space requirements.

The provincial government should encourage the establishment of courses in restoration architecture at the University of Montreal and McGill.

Capital construction grants should be revised in such a way as to permit universities to upgrade the architectural standards of new construction.

The role of the provincial government in the destruction of Montreal's heritage hasn't always been passive. Some of the most devastating projects were provincial schemes, such as the east-west autoroute which was directly responsible for the loss of a number of fine religious buildings.

Ordinary citizens have no recourse against such projects, and no method of appeal. Expropriation laws are all-powerful and it is almost impossible to stand against them and win.

The provincial ombudsman should have the power to intervene and to order public hearings in cases where government development programs threaten neighborhoods or valuable buildings.

The federal government, too, has a part to play, especially in the area of taxation. Tax laws as they stand now provide no incentives for restoration work and actually militate against the preservation of older buildings through the method of determining capital cost allowances and the provisions relating to recaptured depreciation. Unless these are changed, it will remain in the financial interests of an individual or corporation to demolish an existing building and to construct a new one, instead of attempting to save older structures.

Federal income tax laws should be amended so as to make gifts of cash or property to organizations like Heritage Canada more attractive.

Federal corporation tax laws should be changed so as to provide incentives for the preservation of older buildings rather than for their demolition.

Individuals spending money for bona fide restoration of historic buildings should be allowed to deduct such sums from income tax.

The federal government should establish a program of grants, subsidies and loans for purposes of restoring historic buildings.

The federal government could also make some move to put its own development house in order. Projects like Place Guy Favreau and the CBC building in the east end have devastated well-established Montreal neighborhoods. Yet, as in the case of the provincial government schemes, affected citizens have no recourse.

The federal government should set up a special review board empowered to hold public hearings into all federal development projects to which there is substantial public objection.

The federal government should reorient its development priorities in order to put emphasis on the recycling of older buildings wherever this is feasible and desirable.

The governments aren't the only ones with a role to play, however. Every Montrealer has to participate, if the city is not to be lost by default.

Ordinary citizens concerned about preservation can join one of the groups aligned with Save Montreal, circulate petitions, or simply draw the attention of the press, the Viger Commission, and their city councillor to threatened buildings.

Tenants have a more active role since the coming into force of the new Quebec Rental Act in January, 1974. The law protects them against eviction by a landlord who wants to demolish a building as long as they retain a valid lease. This particular provision was instrumental in the saving of four fine mansions on McGregor in the summer of 1974. By invoking this right before the rental board, tenants in threatened buildings can win stays of execution which may eventually result in the building being spared.

Unless Montrealers exercise the rights and the power they hold as ordinary citizens, the destruction of the city's heritage will certainly continue. What will eventually emerge will be a bright, shiny collection of high-rises and underground shopping centers—attractive, but completely unrelated to the city's historic past; a rootless series of high-priced shells.

The alternative is a city which holds simultaneously to the past and to the future; where well-planned new projects coexist with recycled reminders of other times, and familiar landmarks provide a sense of comfort and continuity.

Only the people of Montreal can make that happen. We are all standing at the crossroads.

Where to turn for Help

Government and Government-sponsored Bodies
Responsible for Preserving the Canadian Heritage

Canadian Inventory of Historic Buildings
Begun in summer, 1970, this nation-wide computerized survey is the first of its kind in the world. It was started under the auspices of the National Historic Sites and Monuments branch of the federal Department of Indian Affairs and Northern Development. The survey is divided into three phases. Phase I recorded exterior details of 100,000 buildings. Phase II, now in progress, involves examining in detail the interiors of the best 5,000 of those 100,000. Phase III will weed out the most outstanding buildings for consideration for classification by the federal government. Director of the inventory is Meredith Sykes, a graduate of Columbia University's architectural preservation program.

Cultural Property Commission
A 12-member body which advises the Quebec Minister of Cultural Affairs. The Commission was created by the 1972 Cultural Property Act and is headed by Georges-Emile Lapalme.

Montreal at the Crossroads

Heritage Canada
Headquartered in Ottawa, this organization was created with a
$12 million federal grant in April, 1973. It is now independent
of the federal government and its annual income is derived from
interest on the grant. Director Robert A.J. Phillips hopes the
organization will be Canada's answer to Britain's National
Trust. Heritage Canada publishes a quarterly magazine but does
not buy buildings. Its aims are heritage education and pressure
for better preservation laws.

Ministry of Cultural Affairs
The Quebec government body charged with preservation of the
province's cultural heritage. Classification of a property by the
Minister of Cultural Affairs prevents its sale or demolition without government permission.

National Historic Sites and Monuments Board
A 13-member advisory body, created in 1919. It is part of
Parks Canada and advises the federal Minister of Indian Affairs
and Northern Development. The Board can authorize purchase
of national historically important buildings. It can also buy
property in cooperation with other organizations and erect plaques on important sites. It does not, however, have power to
protect any site from demolition.

Viger Commission
A 21-member group created by the City of Montreal and the
Quebec government and named for Jacques Viger, the city's
first mayor. Its specific responsibility is the historic quarter of
Old Montreal but it also acts as an advisory group on historic
buildings throughout the city. The Commission reports to the
Montreal City Planning Department.

Montreal Citizen Groups

The addresses and directors of the groups listed
below may change in the future, but the list
will continue to provide a good point of
departure; also, the citizen may refer to Save
Montreal, the peak organization to which all
the groups belong, for further information.

Bishop Street Tenants Association
Stuart Reed
Box 326 Station H
844-5598

Canadian Heritage of Quebec
Colin J.G.Molson
2025 Peel St.
481-5796

Comité des Citoyens de Rivières des Prairies
Jacques Leblanc
Collège St. Jean Vianney
14800 Gouin Blvd E.
Rivière des Prairies
648-6961

Comité de Conservation de Montréal
René Boulay
666 Sherbrooke St. W., Apt. 1607
Montreal
842-1895

Community Design Workshop
Joseph Baker
1087 Greene Ave.
392-5423

Conservation Society of McGill University
Write in care of McGill Student Union
Attention: Lisa Lewis

Esplanade Residents Association
Peter Wedd
4085 Esplanade ave.
861-9901

Faubourg Cherrier
Roger Gratton
3676 Rue St. Hubert
844-6613

Friends of Windsor Station
Michael Fish
4920 de Maisonneuve Blvd.
486-8395

Greene Avenue Village Association
Joanne Issenman
493 Elm Ave.
932-7659

Green Spaces/Espaces Verts
Denise Faille
247 Melville Ave.
932-7422

Griffintown Peoples' Association
Terry Coady
222 Mountain Street
932-4877 or 932-6783

Haddon Hall Tenants Association
George Seaden
2150 Sherbrooke St. W.
845-0238

216

Human Rights for Senior Citizens
John E. Pierson
250 Ontario St., Apt. 5121
845-3798

Logeantoine
Bob Stanley
430 Prince Arthur St., Apt. 6
842-8836

Lower Westmount Citizens Committee
Fred Leclaire
3209 St. Antoine St.
931-3166

Milton Park Citizens Committee
Lucia Kowaluk
3703 Jeanne Mance St.
844-4076

Montreal Society of Architecture
Pierre Beaupré
1825 Dorchester Blvd. W.
866-4003

Save the Main Research Committee
Brian McCarthy
3892 St. Lawrence Blvd.
842-8836

Society for the Preservation of Great Places
Michael Berger, Q.C.
3410 Peel St., Suite 2102
288-4177

Somerset-Lincoln Street Tenants Association
Aurelien Guillory
2082 Sherbrooke St. W., Apt. 6
933-9449

Montreal at the Crossroads

Stanley Street Committee
Mark Elvidge
3483 Stanley Street
288-8574

St. Hubert-Carré St. Louis Association
Michel Laville
3435 St. Hubert Street
522-2087

St. Urbain Community Center
Dimitri Roussopolis
University Settlement of Montreal
3553 St. Urbain Street
842-7432

Students Society, McGill University

Terrasse Ontario
Louis Pretty
343-7503

Save Montreal/Sauvons Montréal
Peter Lanken
P.O. Box 123
Montreal
844-2266

CRISE (Centre de recherches et d'information sur
l'environnement)
3577 de Buillion
843-5065

Bibliography

Books and Publications

Annual report, Quebec Ministry of Cultural Affairs. Quebec, Official Publisher, 1973.

Canadian Building Magazine, Vol. 24, No. 5, pp. 25-27, Toronto, MacLean-Hunter Ltd., May 1974.

Jacobs, Jane. *The Death and Life of Great American Cities,* New York. Vintage Books, 1961.

La Haye, Jean Claude. *Rapport La Haye,* Quebec, Government of Quebec Printers, 1968.

Lorimer, James. *A. Citizen's Guide to City Politics,* Toronto, James Lewis and Samuel, 1972.

McGill University Senate Committee on Development. Eighth Progress Report, McGill University, September 1972.

Montreal Urban Community Planning Department. Proposals for Urban Development, Montreal, 1973.

Proceedings of the 114th Annual Synod, Diocese of Montreal, Anglican Church of Canada. May 25, 1973.

Quebec Cultural Property Commission. First annual report, Quebec, 1973.

Richardson, Boyce. *The Future of Canadian Cities,* Toronto, New Press, 1972.

Windsor Station/La gare Windsor. Friends of Windsor Station, Montreal, 1973.

City By-laws

Montreal City Council. A by-law to create a planning department. No. 2593, Jan. 16, 1961.

Montreal City Council. A by-law to create a city housing department. No. 3545, Nov. 27, 1967.

Montreal City Council. A by-law to regulate height of buildings on the side of Mount Royal and prevent view of mountain from being obscured. No. 3722, Sept. 30, 1968.

Montreal City Council. A by-law to amalgamate the municipal housing and planning departments into one body, and requiring the department to maintain a master plan for the city and a list of historic sites to be preserved. No. 4369, Jan. 25, 1972.

Montreal City Council. A by-law to limit the floor-area ratio of residential buildings in the downtown core. No. 3411, Feb. 18, 1974.

Provincial Laws

Quebec National Assembly. A bill to establish a Cultural Property Commission and to authorize the Minister of Cultural Affairs to recognize or classify cultural property. Bill 2, 29th Legislature, 3rd session, July 8, 1972.